Mary Wald has been writing, editing, and producing media with Nobel Peace Prize laureates, including former Presidents Mikhail Gorbachev and Jimmy Carter, Archbishop Desmond Tutu, and His Holiness the Dalai Lama, for more than two decades. She is the international media representative for José Ramos-Horta, 1996 Nobel Peace Prize laureate and current President of Timor-Leste.

ID have to find out what I should do with it.

"No," said Anna.

"No? What do you mean?"

"I mean I don't believe it. What is this — some kind of a trick?"

Vera looked taken aback. "No trick. I've thought it over and I've made up my mind. I don't want any more trouble."

"You're lying," Anna said.

"I'm not. And I must say, I don't understand why you're being so unpleasant about it."

"I'll tell you why. Because I don't believe you. You wouldn't give up like that. Not you."

Vera shrugged her shoulders. "You needn't believe me, my dear, but I assure you it's the truth. I've finished with the whole thing. I've decided to leave Berlin."

"Oh?" said Anna. "Where are you going?"

"I haven't decided yet. Perhaps back to Vienna. Or perhaps to Paris. I have friends in both places."

"I see." Anna's voice was flat with disbelief.

Vera gave her a long, searching look. "You don't trust me, do you?"

"No," said Anna.

"Well, perhaps I can't blame you. But it's the truth, all the same."

"Prove it," said Anna.

"How?"

"Give me back the letters. All of them."

Vera laughed. "Oh, come now, Anna. You can't expect me to do that. They're my only protection."

"Protection against what? If you're really leaving, you won't need protection."

"One never knows," said Vera. "I prefer to keep them."

"Then I don't believe a word you've said."

Vera sighed. "Very well. If that's how you feel, there's nothing more to be said. I only came out of courtesy, to let you know."

She stood up to go.

"Wait," said Anna.

Vera paused.

"What do you really want?"

Vera smiled. "Nothing, my dear. Nothing at all. Good-bye."

And she walked out, leaving Anna staring after her.

SOWING HATE AND CHAOS
How Propaganda is Used to Destroy Democracies

MARY WALD

Marchant Books

marchantbooks.com

© Mary Wald 2024. All Rights Reserved.

Marchant Books supports the value of copyright and its vital role in encouraging and fueling creative works. Thank you for respecting intellectual property and copyright law by not scanning, uploading, or distributing copies of this book without permission. If you would like permission to use material from the book (other than for review purposes) we are happy to discuss possibilities. Please contact permissions@marchantbooks.com. Thank you for your support of the author's rights.

Paperback ISBN: 979-8-9914813-0-4

E-Book ISBN: 979-8-9914813-1-1

Proofread and French translations by Corinne Simon-Duneau

Edited by Tim Rosaire

Cover Photo by Kirstine Rosas on Pixabay

*For those who swim against the current
for the benefit of their fellows.*

CONTENTS

FOREWORD	xi
INTRODUCTION	xix
CH 1: HOW DEMOCRACIES ARE UNDONE	1
CH 2: HOW THE SEEDS WERE SOWN	33
CH 3: PHASE 1: INDOCTRINATION AND RECRUITMENT	55
CH 4: THE FUNCTION OF THE SCAPEGOAT	67
CH 5: GROUPS AND OPINION LEADERS	73
CH 6: PHASE 2: THE PROPAGANDA OF AGITATION	87
CH 7: PHASE 3: THE PROPAGANDA OF INTEGRATION	99
CH 8: SOCIAL MEDIA: PROPAGANDA MEETS BIG DATA	129
CH 9: WHERE WE ARE	157
APPENDIX	183
ACKNOWLEDGMENTS	201
END NOTES	203

FOREWORD
By José Ramos-Horta
President, Timor-Leste, 1996 Nobel Peace Prize laureate

I met Mary Wald in 2001, when I was in San Francisco on a speaking tour. My country, the small island nation of Timor-Leste (formerly East Timor), was emerging from a 24-year occupation, during which a third of our population had perished, most by execution or planned starvation. I was Foreign Minister, helping to shepherd the birth of the millennium's first new democracy.

It was the beginning of a long friendship and working relationship. Mary has acted as my editor and international media representative for more than two decades now. Jointly we have organized my fellow Nobel Peace Prize laureates into actions on critical social issues, which Mary has then released to the international press.

On September 11, 2001, the United States woke up to the

unprecedented attacks against the World Trade Center and Pentagon; Americans watched as more than 3,000 of their countrymen died, including 50 who were killed when they bravely crashed the hijacked plane they were on before it could do further damage. I was in Indonesia, in and out of meetings with then President Megawati. Mary was in Napa, awaiting news on a friend who had been working in the Pentagon. In our conversations that day, amid our mutual shock, we decided to ask the Nobel Peace Prize laureates to respond to the attacks. I emailed my fellow Nobel laureates, and Mary followed up, gathering the statements from 16 Nobel laureates, including Nelson Mandela, Desmond Tutu, Mikhail Gorbachev, Oscar Arias Sanchez, His Holiness the Dalai Lama, and others. She posted the statements to her website, TheCommunity.com, and released them to the international press. Their responses are now in the US Library of Congress archive on the 9/11 attacks.

In the course of gathering the statements, Mary received a fax from Palestine, in Arabic. It was a statement from Yasir Arafat, who had won the Nobel Peace Prize with Shimon Peres and Yitzhak Rabin for the Oslo Accords, yet another attempted peace agreement for the volatile region. Even knowing the controversial nature of Arafat's statement, we were in no position to second guess the Nobel Committee—we included Mr. Arafat.

People coming to TheCommunity.com could email the laureates about their statements. Mary forwarded the statements from the site's readers to the offices of the laureates and acted as a relay for me on matters related to the statements. From this interchange, we were invited to bring a delegation to both Israel and Palestine to support what appeared to be a budding peace process.

By March 2002, I had assembled the delegation, which was to include myself, Elie Wiesel, Northern Ireland's John Hume, South African Archbishop Desmond Tutu, and former President of South Africa F.W. de Klerk. I secured the financing, and Mary secured a media team to travel with us from a leading US news network. While we were still in the planning stages, Mary received a phone call from Mr. Arafat's Chief of Staff. The PLO headquarters in Ramallah had been surrounded by Israeli tanks. It was no longer safe to come.

It is important that we not react too simplistically to these events. This was in the middle of the Second Intifada, five years of heightened violence in both Palestine and Israel. It is an illustration of the extreme complexity of the Israeli-Palestinian conflict, a complexity that even those who have achieved peace and conflict resolution in other areas of the world, and who have been ready to assist, have not been able to help resolve.

Since that time, Mary has continued to support me and Timor-Leste through many phases of the country's growth, including civil conflict from 2006 to 2008. She was with me and my family members when I narrowly recovered being shot by renegade soldiers during that conflict.

I am happy to say that today Timor-Leste is peaceful, and despite lacking the wealth of some of its neighbors, is one of the strongest democracies in Asia. After suffering many of the "growing pains" common to young democracies, today it is an oasis of peace and tolerance, with zero political violence, no ethnic or religious tensions, no armed robbery, and no organized crime.

Having been with me on this road, and through working with other Nobel Peace Prize laureates, Mary has had a close view of life under dictators and occupiers. She has seen the price people in other parts of the world will pay for the kind of democracy and protection of inherent human rights we enjoy today in Timor-Leste. She has known people who fought (and some who still fight) for these rights at risk of imprisonment, torture, and even death. So she must be as shocked as I am that Americans are willing to allow their democracy to be dismantled based on conspiracy theories that are supported by no credible evidence whatsoever— some of which border on the absurd— or out of a contagious hatred of their own countrymen or people of color. Even more baffling to both of us is that so many adore the man who will take it from them, a man who openly dreams of a presidency where all branches of government are subjugated to the desires of the president, where the president operates above the law with impunity, i.e., a fascistic state, a man who openly vows to "root out" the "leftists" he falsely claims are destroying the country and erect concentration camps for brown-skinned immigrants. Perhaps they think it is only the liberals they have come to despise so bitterly who will lose their rights under such a structure. It doesn't work that way.

These events have created a new and very different situation in conflict and peace. As the world's most powerful democracy falters, the American phenomenon has opened the door to other autocrats to follow its path, threatening to drastically alter the shape of our world. It will not be for the better.

I have seen the United States from multiple perspectives. In 1975 I left my country as warships were being loaded in Indonesia in preparation for an invasion that would kill hundreds of thousands of my countrymen. When the ships and paratroopers arrived on our shores three days later, they began executing the members of my political party on the dock, letting their bodies fall into the ocean.

I came to New York in 1975 to plead the cause of my people to the United Nations. We had no allies aside from the Portuguese-speaking countries and tiny Vanuatu. I was treated with open hostility by the US Administration. I was not surprised. US President Gerald Ford and Secretary of State Henry Kissinger had authorized the invasion. As I went forward, I received vital support for our struggle from American Congressmen, particularly Senator Tom Harkin.

President Bill Clinton's election in 1992 marked a change in US policy toward Timor-Leste and the beginning of support for our struggle. In 1999, it was President Clinton who made possible an international coalition called International Force for East Timor, unanimously authorized by the UN Security Council, to be deployed in record time. This peacekeeping force saved the Timorese people from Indonesia-backed militia executing a murderous "scorched earth" campaign as the Indonesian soldiers left the country. I have also worked with and served on the International Advisory Council for the International Republican Institute.

Democracy is imperfect. It is problematic and argumentative. By its nature it brings opposing forces to the table. It was born of arguments—often bitter ones—among the American founding fathers over the power of the federal government vs. state's rights, slavery, the conduct of the Revolution, and post-Revolution foreign policy, among other issues. The system itself rests on the ability to compromise and find common ground.

As we have seen today, the system can be hypocritical and manipulated for the good of the few, while others are left out of the conversation altogether. But it is also the essential basis for peace. One of the examples of this is the 1987 Arias Peace Plan, an agreement between the leaders of Costa Rica, Guatemala, El Salvador, Honduras, and Nicaragua that put an end to the Sandinista-Contra conflict, with a structure for free elections and safeguards for human rights. The Sandinistas were brought into the political process, where they brought their arguments to the table rather than the military arena. Costa Rican President Oscar Arias was awarded the Nobel Peace Plan for his work.

Northern Ireland's John Hume, a fellow Nobel laureate, put an end to the Irish Troubles with a new structure, the Good Friday Agreement, that ensured Catholics in Northern Ireland fair representation and a true voice in the Northern Irish government, something that had been long denied them. When apartheid South Africa threatened to boil over into a bloody civil war, South African Blacks were brought into the political process and granted the vote—bringing their arguments to the political table instead of the burning streets.

Did these result in perfect nations? Not by far. The actions to bring peace are not an end; they can only be a beginning, the start of a long process. After achieving democracy, my own country exploded in civil conflict in 2006. After the end of the Sandinista-Contra conflict, the region was still full of arms and young men trained to torture and kill by the US and the Soviet Union as they used the region as their proxy battleground. South Africa's government has been riddled with corruption scandals. Democracy put these nations on a road that could be a long and tumultuous one. But the alternative to the democratic process, imperfect as it is, is violence and death.

A grave danger to that process, in any part of the world, is the possibility that someone would halt the conversation, that he or she would convince others that the "other side" is so hostile, so evil, so threatening, that one should not cross the line and sit at the table; that the opposing party is, as Donald Trump has said, composed of "Communists, Marxists, Fascists, and Radical Left Thugs that live like vermin... and will do anything possible, whether legally or illegally, to destroy America." When there is no conversation, no table, and no argument, history shows us that the argument will certainly move back to the streets, with arms.

Sowing Hate and Chaos is an invaluable exposé of psychological techniques that have been used to manipulate populations into just that—an end to the argument, an end to democracy, and a violent end to rights and freedoms. It reveals the Godless, denigrating, and manipulating men and women who designed and have implemented the techniques that accomplish this end. And it issues a stark warning—the silencing of voices will be a necessary part of the dismantling of democracy.

I am proud that *Sowing Hate and Chaos* is written by my friend and colleague. But it must be a call to action, to the bright ones, the creatives, the leaders of religions and believers in democracy of all political parties, in the United States, Europe, and elsewhere. *Sowing Hate and Chaos* illustrates that our freedom is clearly not guaranteed. As Artificial Intelligence threatens to increase the capability of the anti-democratic leaders and the manipulators who elevate them, we are increasingly faced today with what may seem frightening but is nonetheless a very real choice. As many in other parts of the world can attest, we can stand for freedom and democracy now, or we can die for it later.

INTRODUCTION

In 2013, I got notice that the 1926 Tudor Revival house I was renting in Pasadena, California, was being sold. The California real estate market was heating up. American, Chinese, and Russian investors were buying up Los Angeles, for cash. Lots of it. And rents were going up proportionally. Especially for charming homes like this one.

I was doing work I loved, but not work that paid well. After 12 years in Los Angeles, if I wanted to keep doing what I was doing, I had to make a jump. After doing some exploring, I decided to settle in California's famous Gold Country, a region of well-preserved small towns nestled in the Sierra foothills that were founded during the Gold Rush. I chose a small town of 700 people on the road to Lake Tahoe, two and-a-half hours east of the San

Francisco Bay Area, where I had grown up. The town is surrounded by wooded hills, with a clear blue river where you can still pan for gold. Everything is authentic, down to the local hotel that has been in business since 1851.

A big selling point for the area was the property prices. I purchased a beautiful two-story Italianate Victorian house that was built in 1890 and located just half a block from the old hotel, for $150,000. I repainted it in historical colors, stripped the floors down to their original Douglas fir planks, and installed a new wood stove, the house's only source of heat. Then I started on the outside, putting in a front yard, pouring a patio under the big fig tree in the back, replacing the fences, and building a deck.

As I completed work on the house, I began settling into my new rural lifestyle. After a life of living in loud, impersonal cities, this was a stereotypical small town. Everybody knew everyone else; they knew who visited you, what time they arrived, and when they left.

With the help of my neighbors, this city girl quickly learned how to build a fire in her new wood stove, where the best ranches were to buy firewood, and how to tell whether it was dry enough to burn by cracking two sticks together and listening to the sound. I began defining "financial security" as having a five-foot-high stack of dry live oak running down the side of my long driveway.

To the rest of the world, California means the areas I grew up in, the San Francisco Bay Area and Greater Los Angeles—beautiful, rich, and blue. You don't hear much about the eastern side of the state. You probably buy strawberries, garlic or lettuce from the farmlands further south.

INTRODUCTION

If there are "fly over" states in the United States, the eastern side of California is "drive through" territory, the way you go when you take Highway 5 from Northern California to LA. The most I could have told you about before moving there was the Chevron station and the In-N-Out Burgers in Santa Nella, about one third of the way down, and the Starbucks at the Bakersfield turnoff, where you get a mocha to take you over the Grapevine pass into LA. You want to make it to that cutoff before the Starbucks closes at 8:30.

Politically, the area is solidly red. But it would be a peaceful environment to write and work, and would still be close enough to two airports to jump on a plane to anywhere. It worked.

My first sign that there was more to the story was a few months in, when I got the first email chain. It had about sixteen recipients. There were four "founding families" of my town, families that had been there for many generations. This was from the matron of one of them. Not only was Obama a Muslim, it said, but Hillary had secretly converted to Islam. They would never leave the White House. This would be the beginning of the Muslim takeover of America unless patriots took up arms to save the nation.

You have a moment when this comes on your email from people you know. It feels like you haven't just landed in another part of your state, you have landed in another universe. And in 2013, who knew this other universe even existed?

There was lots of talk of patriots and arms on Facebook pages. Then there was the notice in the Post Office. A meeting was called to discuss the secret government machines that were creating hurricanes and floods.

I met my first Holocaust denier. I may have met Holocaust deniers in the past without knowing it, but I certainly never knew anyone who would question it out loud. When I made a comment, at my own dinner table, about how Mexicans have played an important part in California, a local woman, who is now on the school board, stood up and started screaming denigrating remarks about Mexicans. I saw a car driving around the "big city" (almost 5000 people!) next to our little town with a bumper sticker that said, "Hey n-----, didn't anyone tell you it's a White House?" The "N word" was spelled out.

Two years into my move, in 2015, my town was in the middle of the Butte Fire, a 65,000-acre wildfire. The town was spared, but just barely. The fire whipped up the canyon around the town three times and was beaten back three times.

This is where all politics goes to the side and small towns shine. The nearby casino set up rows of beds for evacuees and handed out food and water. A veterinarian set up in a field in the next town over for evacuated animals. When the power was out for long stretches we started grilling up our best meats before they could go bad and had some great neighborhood dinners by candlelight or generator. When people from the ranches came back to ashes and mangled metal where their homes had been, the entire town pitched in to help them rebuild. I had furniture in storage that I gave to someone who was setting up a trailer where their house had once been. Everyone did what they could.

Everyone except for the pastor of our local evangelical church. He refused to ask his congregation to donate. The fire, he said, was God's punishment for gay marriage. A neighbor said the fire was thermonuclear warfare being waged on us by the US government. Another said it was created by the United Nations, as part of "Agenda 21," the plot to run people out of the rural areas and into the cities where they could more easily practice mind control on them.

In 2018 in a nearby town, a Jewish man had his house ransacked while he was out of town. Windows were smashed, anti-Semitic hate was etched onto the walls. The invaders urinated on the beds, spilled gasoline, and flooded the house. They painted the name of the neo-Nazi gang from the local high school, "44 gang," into the walls of his living room. Nothing was done by local law enforcement. The US Department of Justice authorized fingerprinting and DNA collection from the site. It was never done.

I mentioned the incident once while in a group of local people. The same woman who had stood up and screamed about the Mexicans at my dinner table said, "Some people think he did it himself, for the money." If this rings a bell, it's the same thing Hitler said about Jews.

The Trump campaign was not noticeable in the streets in 2015 when the fire was happening in our area. There were no huge rallies for him and Trump never visited the Gold Country. His campaign managers must have calculated that he would never carry California, so why waste a lot of time trying. The closest he came was a quick stop in Fresno, a few hours south of the Gold Country, where he told the farmers that the California drought was a hoax and, if elected, he would bring back their water, which of course never happened because there was indeed a drought and he didn't understand the first thing about water rights.

Still, support for Trump was building rapidly in the eastern and northern "drive-through" areas of the state. He was speaking their language and people who believe that forest fires are started by secret governmental agencies don't do a lot of fact-checking. Large homemade banners began appearing in the ranch areas outside of town. "Hillary for Prison" signs also started sprouting up on my neighbors' lawns.

When Hillary Clinton said that half of Trump supporters were a "basket of deplorables"—the "racist, sexist, homophobic, xenophobic, Islamophobic" ones—she was talking about my town, my county, and others like it across the country. But having seen them up close, I don't know how many of the racist, sexist, homophobic, xenophobic, Islamophobic ones are just angry or hopeless and don't know who to hit out at, so they grab whatever group is handed to them at the dinner table, at the bar of the hotel, on chain emails, or on Facebook or Twitter.

So what are they angry about? They're angry because the days when they were superior simply because their skin was white have slipped away, and now they are called "deplorables" by the liberal elites. But it's more than race; they are angry because they have been disenfranchised by the wealthy people in the liberal cities, who dictate the State's policies with their numbers and money. They are angry because in Silicon Valley, two hours away from their homes, they see millionaires and billionaires being minted virtually daily, while they are driving on roads that are in some parts worse than roads in developing nations.

The Gold Country, as well as other regions of northern California, were once supported by mining and timber industries. The mines started drying up in the 1920s; the last large gold mine closed in 1942. The timber industry was first crippled by environmental regulations (literally to save the spotted owl) and then by the arrival of cheaper lumber from China. As one of my neighbors said: "We had jobs. They weren't the best jobs, but we got up in the morning and had somewhere to go. We had health insurance. We had retirement. And our kids had jobs." When the jobs—and the service industries that supported them—went away, no one outside of the region even noticed.

Today, if you live in the Gold Country, your kids graduate high school and leave. They go to Sacramento, Chico, or Lodi to get jobs. Or they join the Army. Some women and men make it in the Army, come home, take a place in the community, and do the area proud. Many don't. No small number come back addicted to opioids and spiral down.

You can say that people in regions like these are not educated. But before you call them stupid, realize that spread up and down the California coast there are more than 158 four-year colleges and universities. Along the Highway 5 corridor in the eastern part of the state there are 15, and two of them are small private Christian colleges.

The one University of California campus in the region, UC Merced, has around 7300 students. The nine other University of California campuses, on the western half of the state? They total about 286,000 students. If you add in Stanford and USC, it's 352,000. And without an education, the doors to Silicon Valley will remain closed to you, while the educated from India and other countries will walk right through.

How hard would it be for the wealthiest state in the nation to open more good colleges in its forgotten half? And perhaps offer some financial assistance for those who want to attend college, but can't afford to? In our fascination with high tech billions and soaring stock prices, how is it possible that no one stopped to take a good look at the other half of the state and said, "Why don't we put something, even a chip manufacturing plant, there?" Instead, they sent the jobs to Asia.

The answer to these questions came to me during a dinner with a former Governor of California. When I mentioned something about the problems the residents of the Gold Country were experiencing, he replied, "Yes but that's just a small number of people." At the time the California budget was running at a multi-billion-dollar surplus. But this would have been the answer of virtually any Sacramento politician over the last decades, and even presidential candidates, who could not be bothered to come to the area. Their focus is on the Bay Area and Greater Los Angeles, where the big voting blocs and donors are.

California's Gold country is far from unique. Similar scenarios have played out in areas across the US where the manufacturing, steel, and coal industries have collapsed, imploding entire regions of the country as the local restaurants lost their customers and people stopped coming to the shops. No one paid attention. As China and Vietnam invested hundreds of billions of dollars in building their clean energy sectors, concurrently retraining personnel from obsolete industries to work in the new sector, the US paid little to no attention to the people being left behind by the exploding new industries and the soaring profits made possible by globalization.

While Hillary righteously "deplored" my neighbors, Donald Trump came to the podium and said "I hear you. And I'm going to nail those bastards who are doing this to you—whether they're Muslims, Mexican immigrants, or Blacks from 'shithole' areas." While many of us laughed at him, derided him, or rolled our eyes, my neighbors were riveted. They had been heard. And they saw a way to strike back.

In September 2016, two months before the election, I wrote an article for *Huffington Post* entitled "Donald Trump's America." The polls were predicting a landslide for Hillary. I said, based on what I was seeing, that I was not so sure. I said there is something happening in America. "It only starts here, when you move away from the blue coast and start to get into rural, red territory. How far, and how deep, it goes, we are about to find out." And find out we did.

As the years ticked on, I worked out how to navigate the Gold Country, and the Trump presidency. I spent many nights working on my computer in front of the fire with my two Tibetan Terriers sprawled at my feet. I stayed anchored to LA and tried to make it down there once a month. I got emails from around the world. I traveled to New York, to East Timor, to Cape Town, Paris, Rome, and Oslo. There was much to love about small town life. When I would come back from out of town in the winter, my neighbor would call and see if I wanted him to start the fire so the house was warm when I got there. On Friday nights the town's residents would gather at the local winery, where we would sit outside with surprisingly good wine, eat from the taco truck or pizza wagon, and sometimes have some nearly decent live music. In the winter we would sometimes huddle on the winery's patio with propane heaters going and blankets over our laps. There were Democrats and Europeans in town. We rotated dinners in our homes and had some real laughs. During COVID we had our own little "bubble" of four or five people so we could keep up our newly established traditions.

During the 2020 election the "Trump Train"—a caravan of close to 100 cars, mostly pickup trucks, honking and shouting, decked out with gigantic Trump banners, including the one with his face superimposed on Rambo's body, came through and stole all our Biden/Harris campaign signs. Someone felt bad later and returned many of them.

Then in December 2020, one of our little social group, a former California Highway Patrolman, mentioned that he had gotten a phone call about a trip to Washington D.C. Some ex-cops were organizing a caravan for January 6 to protest the election results. He didn't go. But as I watched January 6 unfold, I noticed that the people on the rotunda looked and dressed a lot like the people I saw at the local Walmart.

In May 2021, I saw something that made me realize that my nights on my laptop in front of the wood stove were coming to an end. A flier on the Facebook page for our town was promoting a meeting to launch the formation of the "Community Service Militia" for our county. It said that the militia would include, among others, former military personnel, communications specialists, and young/mature adults. They would be taking it upon themselves to provide "assistance and security" in the case of a major earthquake or large disaster, and would be operating in conjunction with the local Sheriff's department. The county Sheriff had been invited to the meeting "to answer questions."

We had been through a disaster. We had made it through with fire crews, and each other. If it happened again, the last thing we would need is armed militia members patrolling the streets. And the Sheriff was going to the rally? I could not shake something I remembered from Timothy Snyder's *On Tyranny*: "When the pro-leader paramilitary and the official police and military intermingle, the end has come."

Four days later, in the next town, I saw an army-green jeep with a mount on top for a very large gun, driven by someone I could have easily mistaken for a meth addict, flying a Three Percenters flag. Then there were more, including one with a Proud Boys flag.

After eight years of small-town life, I did the final fixes on the house, got it ready to sell, and prepared to make another move.

Twenty-two years of working with, and listening to, Nobel Peace Prize laureates has given me a stomach for conflict, and some perspective on how conflicts happen and how they are resolved. One thing that has borne out over and over, in conflicts around the world: hatred, violence and armed civil conflict are not the result of "pendulum swings" or "global shifts."

The Versailles Treaty reduced the once mighty Germany to nearly nothing, leaving German citizens humiliated, fighting hyperinflation, and suffering both a massive unemployment and a dramatic drop in living standards. In the same vein, the economic hardship and exclusion from the benefits of democracy created angry, unjustly humiliated people in large swaths of the United States. No, they weren't pushing wheelbarrows of money around to buy a newspaper. But the financial stability of their regions, their jobs, their futures, were taken from them, in decisions made by millionaires and billionaires in big blue cities—wealthy people who only "flew over" these regions, or in my region of California, passed through on their way to the ski resorts surrounding Lake Tahoe.

But this is only a part of the equation. Armed militia in California (or Michigan, or Pennsylvania, or Oregon) are not natural outcomes of the decline of rural economies any more than Hitler was the natural outcome of the Weimar Republic. The hardship and humiliation created fertile ground. But in every case, and in most of the civil conflicts around our world in the last century, someone had to sow that ground with hatred and aggression. The anger had to be fed and tinged with a thirst for violence that could finally be ignited. Division and civil conflict are engineered by people, not events.

There are steps for doing it. There is a script. It was designed by people who knew how to manipulate, who used lessons learned from fields like "experimental psychology" and "crowd psychology" to develop propaganda that would incite and create violence and chaos. And the script is remarkably uniform from one civil conflict to the next. It has been around for a while. It worked in Germany, and it has worked elsewhere since. Social media opened a new and exponentially more powerful platform for its use.

You often don't know the names of the people who inflame the hatred and violence. You don't really know who is writing or directing the campaigns, the bogus headlines, or the inflammatory speeches. You see their product, spewing crazy into a microphone, leading a campaign rally in a chant, using a flagpole as a spear aimed at a Capitol Policeman on the rotunda of the Capitol, or smashing windows and urinating inside a Jewish center on a college campus. But you don't see them.

Amid the shouting, the shooting, even the killing, these "engineers" are behind the scenes, probably smiling wryly, undetected. From time period to time period, from global hotspot to global hotspot, the end goal of each has been the same: collapse the existing government or system in violent chaos and establish a new order in the nation.

In 1970, a French psychiatrist pulled back the curtain on how it is done, in a 127-page book. If a human rights researcher hadn't discovered it in 1994, the book may have never found its way into public hands. I discovered it almost accidentally while doing research in front of my wood stove one evening.

Never translated, written in obtuse and at times hard to follow academic language, *Psychologie de la publicité et de la propagande* is a handbook for the process. Reading it, I stopped scratching my head and wondering how people I knew could believe the most preposterous things. I understood the emails talking about Hillary being part of the Muslim takeover of America, and the meetings about the secret government weather machines. I understood how my country is being engineered for conflict, violent chaos, and collapse. As it turned out, I had a front row seat.

Chapter 1
HOW DEMOCRACIES ARE UNDONE

As I am working on the final edits for this book, it has been more than two years since I moved from California, and two and a half years since I discovered Roger Mucchielli's *Psychologie de la publicité et de la propagande*, the outline of the methods for creating hatred and violent chaos in nations. In that time, I have been writing, securing the rights to the book, having it professionally translated, making the language of a French intellectual neuropsychiatrist understandable, connecting the dots between events of our last century, Mucchielli's book, and what is happening today, and finally, with the help of two top level editors, producing a final work.

In those two plus years, there have been moments when my heart has raced while typing on the keyboard;

there have been many nights when I have had trouble sleeping after walking away from my computer. I have friends who had trouble sleeping after reading some of the chapters. Reading Mucchielli, and where the road of research has taken me from there, shines a light on the mass manipulation that has been happening right under our noses --- things we have seen but didn't understand. When you understand them, they can be uncomfortable and at times frightening to view.

The most unsettling thing about reading and writing about this is that everything around us is unfolding in pretty much the exact progression Roger Mucchielli wrote about, 50 years ago. Where this progression ends, if he is right, is ugly beyond what we see on the road head of us today. I so want him to be wrong.

Fortunately, Mucchielli also gave us some clues on how to deflate the power of these techniques, meaning the dark clouds ahead of us are not an inevitability. But to deflate them, we have to know about them and understand them.

It is important to know that Roger Mucchielli was no conspiracy theorist writing in a cabin in the woods. He was a French psychologist, a psycho-sociologist, educational psychologist, and neuropsychiatrist. He founded three centers of psychology study and two international journals and was president of the International Institute of Psychotherapeutic Syntheses in France. At the time that he wrote *Psychologie de la publicité et de la propagande*, his son later told me, he was writing a book a year. He wrote this one because he was deeply concerned about the civil conflict in France in 1968, which sent millions into the streets in protest, virtually shut the nation down, and resulted in people being killed in violent clashes. As it does in the US today, the threat of civil war had loomed over their heads. Mucchielli knew what had been done to bring them into the streets and incite them to violence, to get them to try to collapse their own government. He wrote to expose how it was done, in hopes of changing its course.

The techniques Mucchielli describes are not what we normally think of when we hear the word propaganda. This is not the kind of propaganda that selects facts and twists the news, or even the disinformation campaigns that forward lies in national media, documentaries, or books to advance the narrative of leaders. His is a far narrower form of propaganda. It is not working just to change opinions or even votes. It is using psychological techniques to alter thought and behavior. It seeks to shut down the process of reason itself in the person receiving it, and to ignite and inflame a different "mind" in the individual, a much more primitive mind that is driven by old instincts, such as the instincts that cause a herd to stampede or a hive of bees to swarm when they feel the group is being attacked. It lights the fire of these instincts to create a swelling of fear, hatred, aggression, and a thirst for violence, and to then tip that hatred and thirst into violent attack.

These techniques have been used more than once in the last century, in different parts of the globe. Where they have been used, the mobs have been directed toward their fellow countrymen and women, resulting in violent civil conflict.

The ultimate goal of the propaganda is to spin a nation

into chaos, to collapse a system of government, and in the middle of that chaos, to install a new regime. Because it deals with parts of the mind of which we are not aware, our "unconscious" drives, this gets accomplished, according to Mucchielli, with the subjects (us) being completely unaware of the manipulation.

You want to think this sounds like science fiction. But when he describes the steps, they are far too recognizable.

Mucchielli lays out the tools to bring about the collapse, and the installation of the new regime, in three phases. Phase 1 is the Propaganda of Indoctrination and Recruitment. This is the recruitment of the followers, which is done through rallies and through mass communication (in the past radio, today social media), through demonstrations of size and force, hate speech, and scapegoating. Opponents, he says, are mocked, impugned, and accused of presenting malicious, false, or scandalous news. The speeches build the temperature of the hatred by painting a constant threat of destruction waiting outside one's door.

It does not matter if the speech is truthful. In fact, he says that one of the hallmarks of propaganda in Phase 1 is the use of lies that can be easily discredited but continue to be repeated. In Phase 2, the Propaganda of Agitation, the hatred is moved from a thirst for violence to the physical attack. This is accomplished by painting and continuing to reinforce the "reality" around the group members that the forces of evil are gathering, that the battle between good and evil is coming, the ultimate settling of the future, whether it will be in hands of the good and the Godly or collapse into dark at the hands of the evil. It instills the fear of the complete destruction of one's culture, perhaps their religion, the fear that one's values, and all that one holds precious, will be strangled. Once they are fully enmeshed in the "new reality," all that is needed then is to unleash them and direct them where to go. Historically, this has been accompanied by a "catastrophic event" (a fire, an attack, etc.) that has been blamed on the opposition, starting the mass violence. When the violence is sufficient to collapse the nation, the new regime deposes the government and steps in to "restore order."

Phase 3 is after the overthrow, when the new regime is in place. It creates the necessary "uniformity" to cement control by the new leaders, and keep the new regime in power. In this phase the voices of dissent are silenced. Media, the arts, and education are reshaped to fit the narrative of the new regime. Certainly there are no protests in the streets.

There are at least four clear examples where these techniques have been used successfully in the last century: Nazi Germany, Indonesia in 1965-66, Rwanda in 1994, and Myanmar (formerly Burma) from 2012-2017. Of these, the rise of Nazi Germany and Hitler's use of propaganda are the most familiar. Many people don't even know that in Indonesia in 1965-66, roughly 600,000 Indonesians were killed by their own countrymen. A new pro-Western dictator, Suharto, was installed and would remain in power for 30 years.

Between 2012 and 2017 in Myanmar, Buddhist mobs viciously attacked the nation's tiny Muslim minority, the Rohingya, ultimately killing tens of thousands in 2017 and driving more than 600,000 from the country into squalid refugee camps in Bangladesh. The Myanmar violence was engineered by the Tatmadaw, the nation's military, using fake Facebook accounts to incite the hatred and violence. Four years later, when the same generals staged a brutal coup, killing more than 3000 protesters, democracy in Myanmar was dead.

I have included more data on each of these examples in the Appendix for those wanting to do a deeper dive into how they happened. In each case virtually identical techniques were used to incite the mobs and ignite the violence and murder. They used the techniques that Mucchielli laid out in 1970. In Rwanda, the perpetrators of the genocide actually used Mucchielli's book. It was through the work of a Human Rights Watch researcher, Alison Des Forges, that I found the book myself.

Roger Mucchielli did not invent the techniques he writes about. We can see by the techniques and the results that there have been others who certainly knew many of them well, beginning with Hitler and Goebbels.

Documents declassified by the British government in 2021 revealed that the British Foreign Office's cold war propaganda arm, the Information Research Department (IRD), co-operating with right-wing military leaders in the country, had planned and executed the campaign to instigate the mass killings in Indonesia in 1965-66. (See Appendix for more detail). When it was over, celebrating the "elimination" of the Left in Indonesia, the team's leaders boasted that, using limited tactical "psywar measures" and black propaganda, they had pulled off "one of the most successful propaganda operations in postwar British history."

A note in the *New York Times* on October 15, 2018 noted that the officers involved in the Myanmar operation had studied psychological warfare in Moscow. When they came back, they had delivered lectures to others on what they had learned. Myanmar's military had been sending groups of its officers to Russia for military training since 2000.

These examples share another common denominator: in each case the violent mobs attacking their fellow citizens fervently and feverishly believed they were being patriots and saving their nation. They did not use the word "patriot" lightly. In the reality that had been woven around them, they were saving their nations from imminent destruction.

The reason for my racing heart at the keyboard, and my sleepless nights? In the time I have been working on this book, I have watched as the United States has moved from Phase 1 to Phase 2; events in the United States have followed the steps Mucchielli described nearly exactly. The Republican Party has been overtaken by a new regime that has now begun implementing many of the steps for Phase 3, creating "integration" and uniformity of thought within the party, including the banishing and "destruction" of critics within the party, the attempted smashing of candidates who have not pledged allegiance and moved into step behind the leader. (This is easier to do in a political party than a nation). Other areas of society, including some of the nation's largest media outlets, are already in the preliminary steps of Phase 3, and have already begun voluntarily reshaping themselves to the new regime.

As you watch these events unfold in the US through the prism of Mucchielli's work, it presents a very different view. On January 6, 2021, I knew that the mob in the Capitol had been expertly cultivated, primarily through social media, to believe their government was in the throes of an overthrow by the Left, that if they were to save the nation, they must attack. That group was formed and organized by precise steps, not so different from the mobs of violent Buddhists that descended on the Rohingya villages of Myanmar. Some of the language at the rallies could have been lifted out of Mucchielli's book.

That they were attempting to save democracy by destroying one of its bedrocks, the peaceful transition of power, did not occur to those on the rotunda on January 6. Neither did the fact that the claims of voter fraud underlying the "Stop the Steal" campaign had been thrown out in more than 60 court cases. They had been played, skillfully manipulated by people who knew exactly what they were doing. People who knew how to do this had used psychological "tricks" to create a stampeding herd. And stampeding herds don't stop to have their logic questioned.

January 6 was not successful in stopping the transition of power to the elected President. But when you know what to listen for, it becomes very clear—the drumbeat behind the march on the Capitol is growing louder around us every day. Election or no, it will not stop until the new regime is in place.

Does that mean the organizers of January 6 have read Roger Mucchielli? Doubtful. But the fact that you won't find books on Amazon about this kind of propaganda doesn't mean it's not known elsewhere. There are people, both inside and outside the United States, who know what

Mucchielli knew. This is more than evident by their actions. The fact that most have a current or past connection to military intelligence, here or abroad, and that virtually every military intelligence department hires psychiatrists and psychologists, should provide a clue. And now social media has handed them a platform far more powerful than anything their predecessors have known.

The violent mobs created via social media have not been limited to Proud Boys and QAnon shamans. Conflict needs at least two sides. The Black Lives Matter (BLM) protests began as massive, peaceful protests. They devolved into violence, destruction, and looting. There are videos showing people starting the violence in different locations in the United States at virtually the same time, under the cover of night. We can see some of them in the videos, covered head to toe to conceal their identities, while they smashed windows (often with skateboards) and set the violence in motion. Rocks had been stashed nearby for use by the protesters.

In two cases you could see the wrists of the instigators as they smashed windows. They were white. A friend of mine who marched with BLM in Los Angeles saw a group of young men smashing windows and using lighters to try to ignite fires. They were wearing Black Lives Matter t-shirts and masks. They also were white. This friend is a six foot tall Latina, and fearless. She approached one of the group and told him to stop, saying "You know you are hurting the movement." His response? "I don't give a f--- about your movement."

A colleague of mine was in the thick of the BLM protests in Portland, Oregon, when violence erupted. He told me that the protests began, and continued, as peaceful protests in the park, a fact that was almost never covered by the media. At approximately 11:00 p.m., those protesters would go home, he said, and a new crowd would arrive. The 11:00 arrivals were the ones attempting to burn down courthouses and police stations. They also were largely white.

So who were they? You can say they were "Antifa." But who are Antifa? And who has been organizing and directing these people, who were mostly young, to even call themselves Antifa? Some will tell you it's George Soros trying to destroy the US. Some will tell you it's the Right trying to spin the country into martial law to affect a military takeover. We may never know who it actually is. The violence and the mobs were instigated and organized on social media platforms, which provide a cloak of anonymity to the instigators.

The only thing you can say with certainty is that whoever organized these actions, in spots across the United States, knew how to create violent mobs, not so different from the mobs smashing Jewish businesses during *Kristallnacht*, the night of anti-Jewish violence across Germany in November 1938. Not so different from the rioters in France in 1968, smashing windows and burning cars, who would inspire Roger Mucchielli to write *Psychologie de la publicité et de la propagande.*

Between October 2023 and June 2024, there were more than 1300 demonstrations in the United States protesting the Hamas attacks in Israel and the Israeli invasion of Gaza; over 40% of the protesters were students. More than 94% of those demonstrations showed support for the Palestinians.

These also started as peaceful protests until—seeming to spring from the middle of the crowds—someone flashed a swastika to a TV camera. People dressed as Hamas militants with their faces covered called for violence, signs were put up calling for the eradication of Israel. The narrative changed from standing up for the rights, and the lives, of Palestinian citizens, to support for a terrorist group.

On some college campuses this devolved further, into ripping mezuzahs off the doors of Jewish students, smashing the windows of Jewish centers on campus and urinating on the floors. In some cities mobs protested outside of Jewish businesses, or protesters physically attacked Jewish businesspeople. Predictably these have created counter protests and attacks by the Jewish communities, including an incident at UCLA where masked men, who we assume were Jewish, attacked the pro-Palestine students with sticks.

Like the BLM protests, when the violence started, the peaceful protesters would go home. It was two different groups of people. And like the Black Lives Matter violence, the violence and antisemitism that infiltrated the movement to defend the human rights of Palestinian citizens were coordinated and organized on social media, by people who operate anonymously, through accounts that are more likely than not fake identities. Fox News has said, with no evidence, that Soros and other "left wing billionaires" were behind it. The only evidence it showed with the story was a set of figures on contributions to the Biden campaign. The fact that Soros is Jewish was explained on Fox News recently as his "playing both sides of the conflict." The left has accused the right of engineering the violence to discredit the movement and sway Jewish voters to Trump, also without evidence. All we can say with certainty is that we don't know what the real truth is.

As long as they are allowed to operate with anonymity, we may never know who the actual instigators behind the violence are. There are certainly instigators within the United States. There are also powerful groups and governments outside our borders who stand to benefit on many fronts by conflict or chaos in the United States. China and Russia both stand to benefit geopolitically by conflict or chaos in the US. Both have been credibly found to be using fake social media accounts to sow disinformation to influence American elections. It is well-documented in the 2019 Mueller Report that Russian operatives used fake American identities to not only spread influence campaigns and falsehoods on the US election, but even to organize political events in the US through covert operatives. Senator Mark Warner, Chairman of the Senate Intelligence Committee, said in April 2024 that the threat against US elections by Russia and other foreign powers is far greater today than it was in 2020, as adversarial countries have become more adept at creating and disseminating false information, aided by the use of Artificial Intelligence.

In May 2024, *NewsGuard* and the *New York Times* reported on a network of 167 Russian disinformation sites—many with names that mimic American news organizations but forwarding Russian propaganda and fabricated stories—run by a former deputy sheriff in Florida who has now been granted asylum in Russia.

Also in May, Tik Tok released a statement saying they had disrupted 15 "influence operations" working to influence political discourse in target audiences and influence elections, just in the first four months of 2024. The company reportedly removed more than 3000 fake accounts being run by the operators.

Israel's military has admitted to using fake social media accounts to forward the Israeli narrative since at least 2021; in June 2024 the *New York Times* reported that Israel's Ministry of Diaspora Affairs had ordered an operation that used hundreds of fake social media accounts to influence US lawmakers and targeted American audiences with pro-Israel messaging. The campaign also created three fake English-language news sites featuring pro-Israel articles.

At the same time, Iranian operators have distributed fake or falsely attributed videos and antisemitic posts glorifying and excusing heinous war crimes against Israeli citizens that have reached tens of millions of viewers on social media, spurring and forwarding even more antisemitic comments and agreement.

In June 2024, five months before the US 2024 election, Nate Fick, The State Department's top digital and cyber policy official, said that most Americans are seemingly unaware of how much of their day-to-day social media content is actually made up of veiled foreign operatives. "One thing that strikes me is—after a couple of years in this role—I don't think most American citizens really viscerally understand how much of the content they see on social platforms is actually a foreign intelligence operation."

Further obfuscating the source, as you will see in the

following chapters, there are agencies abroad that perform "propaganda for hire," that have worked to influence elections within the US and in other parts of the world. One of these, "Strategic Communications Lab Elections," or SCL Elections, in the UK, was formed by people who had been previously contracted to provide "psyops" for British intelligence. They boasted that they had used online propaganda and psychological manipulation to interfere in elections in more than 60 countries. Another, established and run by a former Israeli military official, brags that his company has 30,000 bots and has interfered in 30 elections worldwide, "27 of them successfully."

I don't know how many agencies there are like these, and of course they are not forthcoming with the details of their operations. The two above were exposed, one by two whistle blowers, the other by a group of industrious European journalists operating undercover. Both agencies were established by men who took "skills" learned through connections and access to military intelligence into the private arena. Both were funded or hired by billionaires who had no compunctions about using dirty psychological tricks to install governments that would be favorable to their private agendas. The most obvious of these was Cambridge Analytica (there is more on them in Chapter 8), which was started by the men behind SCL Elections, with Steve Bannon, and a $15 million investment by hedge fund billionaire Robert Mercer, to influence the American election in 2016 in favor of Donald Trump.

What do the people using these tools have in common? From autocratic governments to libertarian billionaires, they share a contempt for democracy, for the power of the individual citizen. They prefer the top-down power or autocracy over the bottom-up power of democracy. They are all served by the weakening and undermining of the American government. And the man who in his last term in office appointed a Secretary of Energy who campaigned to get rid of the Energy Department, a Secretary of Education who advocated against the public schools system, a head of the Environmental Protection Agency who had a record of suing the EPA, who has weakened America's traditional military alliances and threatens to unravel NATO, is just the man for the job. They all stand to benefit in concrete ways if he brings it all down.

So how do we protect our democracy from the onslaught? As a first action, we can begin to understand the shape of this new weapon being used against us, to recognize it when it comes across our plate, and not be swept into its vector. We need to learn the language and know what is behind it; to know, for example, that when a politician repeats easily discredited lies, it is not evidence that the speaker has a "psychological disorder." It is entirely deliberate. They are painting an entirely new and different reality around the individuals listening to them, one where they and those who echo them are the sole source of truth, where being the dictator of reality makes it possible for the propagandist to direct their reactions and behavior. While from the outside it may sound preposterous, this language is not an anomaly. It is a technique, with a purpose. Know that when the slogan changes from an ideal, such as "Make America Great Again," to a watchword, a call to action such as "Save America," as it did on January 6, the propaganda campaign has shifted from Phase 1, Recruitment and Indoctrination, to Phase 2, Agitation. Violence is coming. And know, the end of Phase 2 is not an election. It is an overthrow.

You may find your heart racing, as I did, as you read some of this material, as the realization settles in of what has been happening in the United States, and the road our country has traveled for more than a decade. There is too much that is too familiar. And where this road goes is unlike anything we have seen or even envisioned in our lifetimes.

I believe it is important to add that the conflict that is being set up in the United States is not a conflict of Democrats vs. Republicans. It is not a conflict of conservatives vs. liberals. Many lifelong Republicans have watched their party disappear, only to be replaced by extremists, as the rhetoric of conservatism and fiscal responsibility has been replaced by denigration, hate, and incitement to violence. The history of their party has been virtually erased, along with its former heroes, including Ronald Reagan. Similarly, lifelong Democrats have been horrified to see people, in the name of "the Left," attack Jewish businessmen or burn and loot stores. The struggle today is not Right against Left. It is democracy against chaos, hatred, and violence.

I am encouraged by the fact that the psychologists who understood and wrote the bases for this virulent form of propaganda also said, more than once, that its power lies in its being undetected, that it works on people who are unaware of the techniques being used. They said that when people know the techniques, that they will reject the manipulation. We can deflate its power by shining the light of day on it. How we do that will be up to us.

Chapter 2
HOW THE SEEDS WERE SOWN

"The conscious and intelligent manipulation of the organized habits and opinions of the masses is an important element in democratic society. Those who manipulate this unseen mechanism of society constitute an invisible government which is the true ruling power of our country." –Edward Bernays, nephew of Sigmund Freud, 1928

You may have never had a conversation with someone who earnestly explains to you that the forest fires in California are being set by the United Nations as part of their secret agenda to run people out of the rural areas and into cities where they can better practice mind control on them. I have. If you live in a liberal city, you probably also haven't tried to talk with someone who believes that JFK Jr. faked his death and is coming back to be Donald Trump's running mate to lead the Great Awakening.

It's an odd experience for someone who loves to jump in and argue a point. I find I have nothing to say. I can only nod and say, "All right."

If you are baffled or confused by their words, it's because you are trying to apply reason. The people who believe these things are talking to each other, not us, and what they are saying has nothing to do with logic.

The ones originating the conspiracy theories, and who continue to fuel them online, know exactly what they are doing. And one of the first things they are doing is methodically shutting down rationality in their listeners.

It is important to recognize that this is not the case with every conversation with people from the opposite political party. The fact that someone votes for, or supports, a candidate you don't like doesn't mean they have had their capacity for reason switched off. Political landscapes are not so simplistic. On one side of that spectrum there are people who vehemently disagree with policies and actions of the other party. This can be rooted in fact. They can be influenced by talking heads and politicians who support, justify and further disinformation or division for more cynical reasons, such as furthering their positions in Congress or the media.

There are those who support propaganda for their own financial gain. Hitler's rise to power was supported by German big business, a support that probably had little to do with his rallies in the squares or even hatred of Jews. Fritz Stern in *Foreign Affairs*[1] describes the wealthy businessmen who contributed to the rise of Hitler as people who "shared with other members of the German elite a nondemocratic bias, a remarkable degree of political illiteracy, a self-assured civic amorality." If that reminds you of Elon Musk, you are not alone.

Privately, it is doubtful that many, if any, Congressional or business leaders honestly believe today that the

2020 election was stolen, or that Donald Trump was the rightful President of the United States in 2021, after more than 60 court cases challenging the election were lost or thrown out of court. But these leaders were not the people storming the Capitol on January 6, 2021. The Congressional members were shuttled to safety by security forces, while wealthy donors and leaders of think tanks who had helped to bring our country to this point were more likely watching the events while safe and warm behind elegant walls.

Those who have wandered from reality are a different category. These are primarily the subjects Roger Mucchielli writes about. In the United States today they include people for whom democracy has not worked out, who have been left behind or ill-served by liberal democracy, who have come to believe that an autocratic government—one that is on their side—will serve to correct the injustices they have received. There are others who believe that a strong leader, even if anti-democratic, will protect them and keep them safe from undesirables and the waves of brown skinned immigrants and terrorists who they believe are flooding across our border to steal our jobs. These are the people that Mucchielli calls "permeable" to this form of propaganda.

These are the people being primed for violence, either to play a part in the violence, or to quietly accept its inevitability. On one level are the people who truly believe that the global elites drink the adrenalized blood of children, and that Donald Trump has secretly released tens of thousands of children from secret underground tunnels where they were being held for human trafficking. On another level are those who have become sufficiently convinced that the opposition is so bent on destroying the nation that they will support a candidate they know intends to dismantle their democracy as a necessary compromise for survival.

Then there are the people behind the scenes—the truly dangerous ones— the practitioners of propaganda, who Mucchielli says draw their power from being undetected; inventing, promoting, and fueling the tales. These are people who will benefit from the United States exploding in civil conflict. Or they work for someone who will.

So how do you get someone to wander down the road of fantastical claims and wild assumptions? According to Mucchielli the first obstacle faced by the propagandist who wants to foment violence is that virtually all civilized societies have common values, which generally include not doing physical harm to one's neighbors or countrymen. We all have built-in brakes against smashing someone else's businesses, burning their home, or picking up a weapon and attacking our neighbor. One of the most cherished fundamentals of Christianity, the Ten Commandments, prohibits both murder and bearing false witness.

The challenge to the propagandist is how to neutralize those brakes that allow societies to function in a civilized manner. Or, as Mucchielli puts it, "the barriers that reason and moral conscience put in the way."[2] There is a way to do this, and it has been around for a long time.

Before we go further down this road, I should add a warning: this chapter is not an easy read. It is about men (and yes, they were all men) who measure us and examine us and draw conclusions about us on the basis that we are little more than a brain, spinal cord, and neurons, with some additional animated matter, responding to stimuli, able to be conditioned and programmed at will. Some of it is incredibly racist, much of it is demeaning. But it was the work of these men that laid the foundation for the worst possible use of propaganda. Knowing about them is valuable knowledge and allows you to recognize when you see them or others of their school at work. Just don't expect them to be fun or colorful people. If it's any consolation, I have had to read much more of them than you will have to.

Personally, I believe the stimulus-response and strictly behaviorist model of humans is flawed, that it does not account for free will, which more than 70% of our world's religions believe is God-given, or the power of the spirit. The behaviorist model does not explain or recognize joy; it discounts it as "manic" behavior. It does not explain the effect on a being of beautiful music, much less the inspiration behind the creation of a symphony, or any number of moments that create beauty in our world. It reduces love to a genetic drive, and uses words like "infantile fantasy" to refer to religion, which to me are the words of someone who does not understand the concept of, and has certainly never experienced, grace.

The strongest evidence of the flaw is that if what these men believed about us was the entire story, their techniques would work on everyone; we would have uniform Orwellian societies by now. We don't. At the same time, I can't deny that these techniques clearly work on some and not others. I don't profess to know why. So let's dive, and I will try not to drag you into too many pits.

THE BEGINNINGS

The word "propaganda" was coined in 1622, when Pope Gregory XV used it to describe missionaries propagating the faith abroad. But even before that, propaganda has been around by other names for as long as rulers and leaders have needed to incite mobs, or citizens needed to be rallied to send their sons to face death in a war, convinced that they were on the side of right and were protecting their lands and their families against the threat of evil. Whether true or not, claiming the cause is just has always been part of the equation.

THE BIRTH OF EXPERIMENTAL AND BEHAVIORAL PSYCHOLOGY

The study of the mind and human behavior goes back to the ancient civilizations of Egypt, Persia, Greece, China, and India. In the West, until the mid-1800s, psychology, the study of the soul (psyche) was housed in the philosophy departments of universities, where lectures and courses included subjects such as immortality, ethics, and higher order of reason.

That all changed in 1874 at the University of Leipzig, in Germany, when Wilhelm Wundt, the first person to call himself a psychologist, established a laboratory to study the brain, neurons, and minute responses to stimuli. With the opening of Wundt's lab, psychology was reshaped as a physical science, focused on those physical characteristics, systems, and responses that could be measured with instruments.

Because they are not measurable, self-determinism, free will, the spirit, those things that made up the psyche, disappeared from the equation. "We speak of virtue, honor, reason;" Wundt said, "but our thought does not translate any one of these concepts into a substance." And substance was all that mattered.

Agreement on Wundt's approach, and the drastic reinterpretation of the study of mind, was far from universal. His own students at times bitterly disagreed with his work. What's important about 1874 in Germany is who *was* listening. PhD students from Europe, Russia and the US flocked to Leipzig to study in Wundt's lab. As they graduated, they went back to their universities to establish departments focused on this new field. British psychologist Raymond Cattell, who authored more than 500 research papers, and established the psychology labs at Pennsylvania and Columbia, and later joined the Harvard faculty, was an early researcher in Leipzig. (Cattell later became a controversial figure due to his friendships with, and intellectual respect for, white supremacists and neo-Nazis).[3] Edward Scripture, a student of Wundt, established the experimental psychology lab at Yale University, and was a founder of the American Psychological Association. G. Stanley Hall, an early observer at Wundt's lab, earned the first doctorate in psychology at Harvard University, and went on to become the first president of Clark University and the first president of the American Psychological Association.[4]

Russian physiologist Ivan Pavlov, who with his dogs launched the field of conditioning, conducted post-doctoral studies in Leipzig from 1884 to 1886, returning to

Russia in 1890 to join the Institute for Experimental Medicine in St. Petersburg. Pavlov was a direct influence on John B. Watson, an early pioneer in behaviorism, the branch of psychology based on the assertion that responses to external stimuli, rather than reason, account for human behavior. (In 1920 Watson famously instilled a phobia of furry objects in an infant using conditioning in his "Little Albert" experiment). He was one of the primary influences on B.F. Skinner, who developed radical behaviorism in the early 1900s, and operant conditioning, which is loosely a process of changing and "programming" 'behavior by offering rewards as positive reinforcement and punishment as negative reinforcement, based on the behavior of rats in mazes, in the 1930s.

FREUD AND PSYCHOANALYSIS

In the late 1890s, Sigmund Freud advanced the behavioral schools further with the discovery of the unconscious and the essential survival drives that apparently control our behavior without our awareness. He divided the personality into three divisions: the id, ego, and superego.

The id Freud describes as a primitive part of the mind that contains aggressive drives, sexual desires, and hidden or unconscious memories. Because it works in the unconscious part of the mind the id is not affected by logic or reason. The two primary drives at this level, he said, are Eros, the drive for love and sex, and Thanatos, which gives us aggression and the "death drive."

The ego is our sense of self, including the functions

such as judgment, synthesis of information, intellectual functioning, and memory. According to Freud the ego is where our thoughts and interpretations of the world lie.

Freud's superego is the part of the mind concerned with moral conscience, with values learned from society and developed as a child grows. The superego controls the impulses of the "primitive" id, particularly those forbidden by society (such as unleashed sexuality or aggression). When a driver cuts you off on the highway, according to Freud, it is the superego that holds you back from flying into road rage. It keeps us from stealing, damaging a neighbor's property, etc.

The ego, according to Freud is the part of the mind that works by reason; is the mediator between the superego (conscience and values) and id (primitive aggressive and sexual drives). And yes, this is a simplification. It is not intended to be a lesson in Freudian psychology.

According to Mucchielli and his predecessors, it was learned from psychoanalysis that the unconscious drives of the "id" have ways of getting around the barriers of morals and conscience. If you want to tap into the "primitive" drives, you speak to and arouse this unconscious "mind."[5] Purposely stimulating this mind and these drives—lighting the fires of these "exploitable feelings" —can create emotional reactions deep enough to cause the person to act in ways he or she would not otherwise act. Knowing how to do this allows someone to direct another's behavior. And it can be done without the person even knowing it is being done.

The first fire, that of love and sex, they say, is lit with the promise of pleasure—happiness, well-being, enjoyment, satisfaction—which provokes desire. This Mucchielli leaves to the advertisers, to sell cars, cereal, and perfume. But it can also be tapped into by the propagandist to create a fierce "love" and unshakable loyalty to a leader.

The second fire, aggression, is lit by building on "frustration (or deprivation, dissatisfaction, suffering, inferiority, humiliation, insult, etc.) which provoke anger, resentment, and aggressiveness."[6] "Aggressiveness," says Mucchielli, is "the fundamental animal and human 'instinct,' and one that can be "considered as registered in the human nature as sexuality." It is the "behavioral expression of emotions such as anger and indignation, of feelings such as hatred, resentment, exasperation."[7] In other words, build enough anger, indignation, and resentment, and the aggression will follow.

How do you light these fires? Not with conversation or discussion. And not by engaging the rational mind. Clyde Miller, an Associate Professor of Education at Columbia University and author of *The Process of Persuasion*, echoed Freud in 1946 when he said that in the "reflex scheme of persuasion, the argument is useless; it is a question of knowing how to handle the symbols, the key words, the images, the ideas." [8]

"It is not necessary to entrust to the individuals the care to think," Miller said. "It is necessary to think for them, to conclude for them, while giving them the impression that they are the ones who thought and who arrived freely at the conclusion, at the necessity of the immediate action." There are different processes "according to whether one targets the converted, the hesitant or undecided, the neutral, the indifferent, or the adversaries." But virtually all of them share the same basic elements. [9]

THE BIRTH OF CROWD PSYCHOLOGY

In 1895, a professor of psychology at the University of Paris, Gustave Le Bon, published *The Crowd: A Study of the Popular Mind*. In the book Le Bon codified the behavior of people when they are part of a mob. In doing so he spelled out the conditions and steps necessary for the creation of the kind of chanting, saluting, adoring crowds that many of the 20th century's worst dictators rose to power on. Le Bon's writings were in the libraries of both Benito Mussolini and Adolf Hitler.

Today, Le Bon is not a familiar name in the US, even to psychology students. Those who do know of him usually regard him as something of a reactionary crackpot with antiquated beliefs around race, colonialism, and democracy, as well as women's place in society. But in Le Bon's time, *The Crowd* was widely considered a seminal work in the emerging field of social psychology, and a founding work of its sub-field, crowd psychology. Sigmund Freud acknowledged *The Crowd* as a brilliant work and remained friends with Le Bon until his death.

In a crowd, Le Bon postulates, the individual's consciousness "disintegrates" into a collective, and more primitive, state of mind. Under the right conditions, this primitive mind—Freud's "id"—can be managed and manipulated by the careful choice of words, colors, music, and staged events. The result is the igniting of the two most powerful drives of the unconscious: Freud's Eros, and Thanatos. These show themselves, Le Bon said, as the love and adoration for a leader, a thirst for violence, and "absolute certainty in the cause, a belief in their own omnipotence, and a furious hatred of perceived opponents."[10]

The violence of the feelings of crowds, he says, is also increased by the absence of all sense of responsibility, and the sense of impunity. These grow stronger as the crowd grows larger, making it possible for members of a crowd to feel things they would never feel on their own.

> In crowds the foolish, ignorant, and envious persons are freed from the sense of their insignificance and powerlessness, and are possessed instead by the notion of brutal and temporary but immense strength...
>
> Crowds exhibit a docile respect for force, and are but slightly impressed by kindness, which for them is scarcely other than a form of weakness. A crowd is always ready to revolt against a feeble authority and to bow down servilely before a strong one.
>
> Crowds are only cognizant of simple and extreme sentiments; the opinions, ideas, and beliefs suggested to them are accepted or rejected as a whole, and considered as absolute truths. This is always the case with beliefs induced by a process of suggestion instead of engendered by reasoning.[11]

According to Le Bon, crowds reason by association of

ideas, associating even dissimilar things by a thin thread of connection, and by the generalization of particular cases. A single immigrant committing a horrific crime becomes the trope that all immigrants are criminals. "It is arguments of this kind that are always presented to crowds by those who know how to manage them. They are the only arguments by which crowds are to be influenced." He acknowledges that the weakness of the argument can be astonishing to the outsider. But as Le Bon reminds us, one must remember that the arguments presented to crowds are intended to persuade and incite mobs, "not to be read by philosophers."[12]

"An individual in a crowd is a grain of sand amid other grains of sand," said Le Bon, "which the wind stirs up at will." He detailed three key processes that create the psychological crowd:

— ANONYMITY, which provides individuals with a feeling of invincibility and the loss of personal responsibility. This lack of self-restraint allows individuals to yield to the instinctual drives of their unconscious.

— CONTAGION, or the spread of behaviors as the individual sacrifices his or her personal interest for the collective interest.

— SUGGESTIBILITY is how the contagion is achieved. As the crowd begins to operate as a "singular mind," rational process is no longer engaged. Think of herds or beehives. Suggestions made by strong voices in the crowd speak to the unconscious (the "primal mind") and guide the crowd's behavior.

Unsurprisingly, neither Wundt, Freud, nor Le Bon were

fans of democracy. Like religion, they considered them the fantasies of past eras. Le Bon referred to Christian beliefs and democracy as "somewhat sorry errors" of the past,[13] and called democracy the dream of "vulgar mediocrities."[14]

> No doubt the weak side of universal suffrage [the right to vote] is too obvious to be overlooked. It cannot be gainsaid [denied] that civilization has been the work of a small minority of superior intelligences constituting the culminating point of a pyramid, whose stages, widening in proportion to the decrease of mental power, represent the masses of a nation. The greatness of a civilization cannot assuredly depend upon the votes given by inferior elements boasting solely numerical strength. Doubtless, too, the votes recorded by crowds are often very dangerous.[15] (Brackets added).

Le Bon exhibited an even darker side in his writings. In the 1870s, before publishing *The Crowd*, he traveled across Europe, Asia and Africa to study the different races. He returned home believing that he had definitively discovered the scientific reason for the superior intelligence of some races over others: the size of their heads. Le Bon supported this discovery by taking along a portable "cephalometer" for measuring human heads.

The concept that the inferiority of some races was inherent and irreversible was not new. For centuries, colonial empires had been built, thrived, and became immensely wealthy on the belief in the inherent and unchangeable superiority of some races (usually the one with the lighter skin) over others. The agriculture of the American South was founded on it. But Le Bon proclaimed this belief was now supported by science and was as unchangeable as the structure of the atom. He was steadfastly against the education of "inferior" races and was even against their being fully included in any society. "If races are dissimilar," he said, "no blending is possible. They may in an extremely strict sense, live side-by-side, like the Hindus in India, who are subject to the Europeans; but one would not dream of providing them common institutions."[16]

The other option is the extermination of the inferior race:

> There are races such as the Tasmanians, where one is unaware of more than a single representative; and it will soon be the same with the American Indians. All inferior people placed in constant contact with a superior people are condemned to perish. It is always by means of systematic and bloody extermination that an inferior people will disappear upon contact with a superior people; the simple action of presence—in order to employ a chemical term—is sufficient to bring about the destruction.[17]

It is no surprise that Hitler drew from Le Bon while writing *Mein Kampf*.[18][19]

And women? This father of social psychology believed that females "represent the most inferior forms of human evolution" and are "closer to children and savages than to an adult, civilized man." [20] His proof, of course, was in the size of their heads.

CROWD PSYCHOLOGY MEETS PROPAGANDA

In the first decades of the 20th century, while some attempted to clarify the unconscious drives in order to reduce their power, others, seeing the explosion of the new sciences of the mind, asked a different question of the work. Edward Bernays, a nephew of Freud, asked it first: "If we understand the mechanism and motives of the group mind, is it now possible to control and regiment the masses according to our will without their knowing it?" [21]

Bernays was living in the United States at the time of World War I, working as a press agent, and spending holidays in Europe with his uncle and family. When the US entered war, he joined the US Government's Committee on Public Information, America's first state propaganda agency, to engineer the campaigns that would stir up support and overcome the opposition of a pacifist population to US involvement in the war by broadly painting the US military as making the world safe for democracy. He proved to be so skilled that, at 26 years old, he was invited to accompany President Woodrow Wilson to the Paris Peace Conference.

After the war, Bernays established a practice in New York, called himself a Public Relations Counsel—a term he was the first to use—and hired out to manufacturers to help sell commodities by tapping into the newly discovered unconscious desires of consumers, to dictate their behavior, including their purchasing habits. He was nothing if not ingenious, pulling off wildly successful PR stunts and earning himself the title "father of public relations" and a position on *Life Magazine*'s 100 most influential Americans of the 20th Century.[22] With his contemporary, Ernest Dichter, he ushered in a new age of advertising, one marked by selling automobiles as long, power phallic symbols, encouraging women to smoke by the "unconscious" suggestion that cigarettes were "little penises," and suggesting, also unconsciously, that a cigarette lighter could provide "sufficient flame to ignite the sexual act."

Both Bernays and Dichter, and their impact on Western life, are studies in themselves. Dichter went on to apply techniques of psychoanalysis in the invention of the focus group, and literally hid behind a couch to watch young girls, noting what he deemed were their unconscious responses for market research on the Barbie doll. Stories of their escapades and capers make up much of the folklore around the evolution of modern advertising.

Bernays simultaneously took the other fork in the road, continuing his service to the propaganda arm of the US government, including working for the Central Intelligence Agency. And if he tapped into unconscious sexual drives to advertise products, in propaganda he tapped into our deep-seated violent instincts, including protection of the herd against outsiders.

In 1952 Bernays was employed by the United Fruit

Company to protect their assets in its most important banana-growing region, Guatemala. After repeated betrayals, Guatemalans had had enough of having their land stolen and were demanding land reforms to right the wrongs committed by the corporation. The banana pickers were also starting to get big ideas about labor unions.

Bernays engineered a propaganda campaign against the reforms and against the country's new President, Jacobo Árbenz, playing on fears of communist infiltration and the "red scare." Creating a fake newspaper and phony front organizations, he sent anonymous reports to members of Congress, and with his corporate bosses ultimately convinced the US to implement a naval blockade, to bomb the country, and finally to threaten a full military invasion. Árbenz fell, and was replaced by a more corporate friendly Castillo Armas, who quickly imposed a police state, outlawed unions and political parties, closed newspapers, stripped banana workers of their rights, and executed Árbenz's supporters.

Like the psychologists and psychoanalysts whose shoulders he rode on, Bernays' opinion of his fellow men and women was not high. Like the others he was also not much of a democrat, believing that people were essentially too stupid and too driven by unconscious impulses to be allowed to govern themselves or make independent decisions.

While he gave lip service to democracy, the Bernays vision of democracy was a far cry from that of John Locke or Thomas Jefferson. In the Bernays version, which contains recognizable shadows of Gustave Le Bon, the "intelligent minorities" can engineer consent using manipulation and propaganda, and they should, for the benefit of the public.

Propaganda, he said, was the executive arm of this invisible government. "...Whatever attitude one chooses toward this condition, it remains a fact that in almost every act of our daily lives... we are dominated by the relatively small number of persons...who understand the mental processes and social patterns of the masses. It is they who pull the wires which control the public mind." [23]

In the early days of the 20th century, as Bernays was rising, the shape of communication to those masses was also changing. In 1894, Italian inventor Guglielmo Marconi successfully engineered the first long distance wireless transmission system. Just three years later, he established the first radio station. By 1912, radios were being manufactured in the US. No longer did people need to gather in the town square to hear their leaders.

Bernays was quick to adapt the findings of Le Bon and Freud to the times:

> Men do not need to be actually gathered together in a public meeting or in a street riot to be subject to the influences of mass psychology. Because man is by nature gregarious he feels himself to be member of a herd, even when he is alone in his room with the curtains drawn. His mind retains the patterns which have been stamped on it by the group influences.... When the example of the leader is not at hand and the herd must think for itself, it does so by means of clichés, pat words

or images which stand for a whole group of ideas or experiences.²⁴

What has begun in a rally can now be continued and kept alive at home, and even shared with others, by repetition of the same words, slogans, images, emotions, with the same unconscious impact, via mass media.

In his autobiography, Bernays relates how, in 1933, a foreign correspondent for Hearst newspapers returned to the US and told Bernays that he had seen his books in the library of Joseph Goebbels.

> Karl von Weigand, foreign correspondent of the Hearst newspapers, an old hand at interpreting Europe and just returned from Germany, was telling us about Goebbels and his propaganda plans to consolidate Nazi power. Goebbels had shown Weigand his propaganda library, the best Weigand had ever seen. Goebbels, said Weigand, was using my book *Crystallizing Public Opinion* as a basis for his destructive campaign against the Jews of Germany. This shocked me. ... Obviously the attack on the Jews of Germany was no emotional outburst of the Nazis, but a deliberate, planned campaign. ²⁵

In 1935 *Barrons Magazine* linked American and German-style public relations, noting that "Hitler, by making what Bernays calls 'Devils' for the German masses to look down upon, has aroused the acclaim of the more easily swayed masses." ²⁶

Supreme Court Justice Felix Frankfurter warned President Franklin D. Roosevelt against allowing Bernays to play a leadership role in World War II, describing Bernays and his colleague Ivy Lee as "professional poisoners of the public mind, exploiters of foolishness, fanaticism and self-interest."[27] Yet today Bernays continues to be lauded as the "father of Public Relations." His last appearance, one year before his death in 1995, was an appearance on David Letterman.

Le Bon, Bernays, Goebbels, and Roger Mucchielli all recognized that the power of psychological manipulation in propaganda rests largely on it being undetected. In Mucchielli's terms, "One who is manipulated and pushed in a certain pre-established direction must remain unconscious of the real objectives and methods of the persuader. Otherwise he would resist the influence or suggestion and set up automatic defenses against them."[28]

The lives and work of these men is not enjoyable reading. But their work is more relevant to our lives today than we probably care to admit.

Chapter 3
PHASE I: INDOCTRINATION AND RECRUITMENT

Mucchielli differentiates between political publicity and true propaganda. In politics, public relations, advertising, and special events are used to get you to vote for a particular candidate or party in much the same way that marketers create brand loyalty or get you to buy a brand of toothpaste.

The form of propaganda Mucchielli describes has a far more sinister aim. It seeks to collapse a system in violent chaos and install a new regime. It "seeks to impose an explanation of the global situation, an ideological conviction, and to provoke behaviors... It seeks to influence the fundamental attitudes of men; it wants, consciously, and armed with all the psychological techniques, to seize the totality of the psyche."[29] In other words, it tries to take over your thinking and get you to behave as they decide you should—without your being aware of it.

Political campaigns are expected to be based on at least a semblance of truth—carefully selected "facts," yes. But the party leaders are expected to be answerable to what is said and portrayed. In propaganda, all bets are off.

In propaganda, accusation of the opponent, whether true or false, is the rule. As Mucchielli puts it, "an integral part of any propaganda message is the denunciation of the adversary as the embodiment of Evil and Lies... One can accuse the adversary of having the devious intentions which oneself has, one can slander him, attribute to him all the possible vices and hypocrisies... All tricks are allowed and recommended, including the fabrication of forgeries."[30]

INTERPRETATION OF FACTS

Facts do not speak on their own, Mucchielli says. They must be "made to speak." And they must be made to say what you want them to say. This is achieved by "selecting facts, manipulating their context, interpreting their meaning."[31]

This is not new. It is a primary skill of good public relations everywhere—in corporations, political campaigns, and yes, news reporting. That someone selects and manipulates facts doesn't make them a propagandist.

Where the manipulation of facts becomes recognizable as an element of propaganda, according to Mucchielli, is when it is demonstrably false and easily discredited, but continues to be repeated. The other hallmark is the thorough discrediting of all other sources of information that conflict with the propagandist's "truth." They are mocked, impugned, and accused of presenting malicious, false, or scandalous news. After a thorough discrediting of other sources and other interpretations of events, the propagandist and their allies—including those covertly placed inside targeted groups—position themselves as the only true "authority" on what actually happened or was said.

Should an adversary or opponent produce a valid or undeniable fact, says Mucchielli, it should be met with diversion, or the *ad hominem* attack—attacking the character of the speaker and ignoring what he or she is saying. [32]

ACCUSATION

From Mucchielli:

> To blacken the adversary, to be cleared oneself as a result, means that if he is the incarnation of the evil or of the demon or of all the vices of the Earth, then the cause that one defends is in the camp of the universal human values, which include morality, humanity, love, loyalty, the service of the good, the three inseparable banners: FREEDOM, JUSTICE, PEACE.[33]

There are two primary ways to accuse an adversary. The first is an accusation of wrongdoing, presented in such a way as to trigger the moral conscience of the listeners.

He suggests accusing one's opponent of hypocrisy, treason, cowardice, intent to deceive, self-serving and selfish malfeasance, perjury, bad faith, use of force against the law.

The other method, "accusation in a mirror," (a term first used by Joseph Goebbels) consists of accusing one's adversaries of the very thing you are doing, or intending to do, yourself. Someone who intends to start a war, for example, will proclaim his peaceful intentions and will accuse the opponent of warmongering. The one who uses terror will accuse the opponent of using terror. The advantages of the mirror accusation are numerous, including the fact that the other side has a hard time answering them. It removes your enemy's arguments, and cements the reality among your followers that honest people must defend themselves against such people.[34]

In a bit of double speak, Mucchielli notes that "accusations of lies against opponents can be facilitated when one has first injected the public with false information as if it came from those opponents. It will then be easy to demonstrate the lie." [35] In other words, plant false information and say it is coming from your adversary. Then publicize the false information to prove they are liars.

EXPLOITATION OF EVENTS

If the above steps have been done skillfully, Mucchielli says, your opponents, their spokespeople, and the media favorable to them will be so well "blackened" that your own media and spokespeople will have become the interpreters of events. The daily stream of events provides the material for continual interpretation.

The propagandist must know how to seize events, exploit them when it's to their advantage. Sometimes a sensational news item is the adversary's fault. Sometimes they need to be fabricated. Mucchielli gives the example of German SS men disguising themselves as Polish soldiers and "attacking" a German border post, which was used to justify the invasion of Poland. [36]

THE SLOGANS

The slogan condenses the ideas or the purported objectives of the party in a clear, striking formula. Its first function is to rally the party. It doesn't have to reflect the doctrine of the party; it's more important that it speaks to the aspirations of the listener, that it aligns with the audience's motivations. It is then repeated and associated with the emblems and symbols of the party. "The most important thing," Mucchielli says, "is to associate it with the acronyms of the party."[37] MAGA works well.

THE SYMBOLS

The symbol expresses and summarizes the group's entire doctrine in an image or object. As Mucchielli describes it:

It is a sign that refers to a whole, one that evokes by its mere presence: the swastika, the hammer and sickle, the three arrows of the Iron Front... In the propaganda campaign, symbols must be everywhere, as well as the badges and the armbands that carry them, as they continue to assert the presence of the party and its value as the authentic defender of the ideas.[38]

Donald Trump's campaign has virtually usurped the American flag, the most powerful symbol of the nation, by essentially wrapping him in it, in campaign TV ads, campaign literature, and personal appearances. The flag has become so ubiquitous and so entwined in his campaign that, in many areas of the US when you see a house or car displaying an American flag today, you probably assume it is being flown by a Trump supporter.

There is no symbol more emotionally powerful for Americans than the United States flag. In our schools, American children stand with their hands over their hearts and "pledge allegiance to the flag of the United States of America." Our national anthem describes sighting the "Stars and Stripes" as the smoke of battle clears. Who doesn't know the iconic photograph and statue of American marines raising the American flag in Iwo Jima during one of the last battles of the Pacific in World War II? Our national marching tune, as proclaimed by an act of Congress, is John Phillip Sousa's "Stars and Stripes Forever," which is played at every Independence Day celebration across the nation.

The US Flag is so sacrosanct a symbol that a US Flag Code exists to define how it is to be treated. The code states that "No other flag or pennant should be placed above or, if on the same level, to the right of the flag of the United States of America," that "The flag should never be used as wearing apparel, bedding, or drapery...The flag should never have placed upon it, nor on any part of it, nor attached to it any mark, insignia, letter, word, figure, design, picture, or drawing of any nature," and "The flag should never be used for advertising purposes in any manner whatsoever." The US Flag Code also states that "The flag should never be displayed with the union down, except as a signal of dire distress in instances of extreme danger to life or property."[39]

The Trump campaign consistently violates this code, attempting to harness the power of one of our most revered national symbols. His rallies are attended by people wearing American flag leggings, sun visors, shirts, dresses, shorts, their trucks adorned with an American flag with an image of Donald Trump superimposed over the stars and stripes. His supporters have flown the flag upside down to protest an election result, without concern for the fact that it defaces a solemn symbol. Donald Trump's social media profile picture is an image of his face superimposed on the flag.

IMAGES AND BANNERS

According to Le Bon, images evoked in the minds of the crowds are so powerful they can be more lifelike than reality. So images used to provoke an emotional reaction, he says, should be presented with as few words as possible, and with no additional explanation, as "Images of extreme intensity would be quickly dissipated should they be submitted to the action of reflection."[40]

I was reminded, reading this, of the flags frequently seen hanging from the houses and cars near my old home in rural California; the same flags were impossible to miss among the crowds rioting in the Capitol on January 6, 2021.

One was the Confederate flag. California was on the Union side during the Civil War. The other was the Gadsden Flag, a yellow background with a rattlesnake, coiled with its mouth open, ready to strike, with the words "DON'T TREAD ON ME" ("DONT TREAD ON ME" in the original). The Gadsden Flag was designed in 1775 and used by the amphibious infantry in the American colonies and during the Revolutionary War.

Both flags evoke other times of high emotion and intensity, one the arrogance of white supremacy, and a willingness to go to war with your countrymen to preserve your superiority and economic privilege, which for some, evokes a sense of pride and imagined nobility. The Gadsden Flag evokes threat and power to harm, from times when one was willing to die for a cause or kill for the cause of freedom. They are presented with as few words as possible, before anyone can ask, "Wait, freedom from what?"

The black and white flag with one blue stripe, seen in the crowds on January 6, and spotted on the occasional decked-out "pickup truck for Trump," was originally used by law enforcement to signify the "thin blue line" between the public and criminals. It was flown at the services of law enforcement personnel who had died in the line of duty, an intensely emotional experience. It was later flown to show support for law enforcement.

During the Black Lives Matters protests, it was flown by those opposing the BLM protests to say they were on the side of the police. None of those who felt empowered by carrying the thin blue line flag seemed to see the irony of displaying the traditional flag of law enforcement as they tasered members of the Capitol police.

And of course, nothing says "who cares if it makes sense, how does it make you feel?" like the flag with the image of Donald Trump's head on Sylvester Stallone's body in Rambo. It evokes strength, power, and courage; qualities that, according to Le Bon, have the potential of being more lifelike than reality to those who display it. It evokes stronger feelings than the less-flattering images of a man going about the regular actions of public speaking, drinking water, even playing golf. Rambo makes them feel good. And feelings, as opposed to reality, are the point.

THE LANGUAGE

The language of propaganda, Mucchielli says, "will always be that of indignation."[41] This is accompanied by the insistence, and repetition, of "the frustration, the damage, the humiliation, the deprivation, the injustice suffered" by members of the target audiences.[42]

Words should be chosen selectively. Both Mucchielli and Le Bon assert that the actual definitions of the words matter less than the emotional impact they produce. In a particularly sinister observation, both mention that words that are undefined, or that have vague or unknown definitions, can be among the propagandist's strongest tools. If you don't have a definition for a word, it is impossible to engage reason in talking about it. If you don't know that the definition of "socialism" is public ownership of the means of production and natural resources, you can be easily riled up into thinking that Social Security payments, providing meals for school children, or government investment in the health care of its citizens is socialism, which will lead to the ultimate scare, communism, which will mean the destruction of your religion. If you don't know the definition of tyranny, you can be convinced with symbols, flags, and rallies that it would be noble, that you would be a "freedom fighter" if you lay your life on the line to defeat the "tyranny" of the Democratic party.

As Le Bon puts it, "Words whose sense are the most ill-defined are sometimes those that possess the most influence…A truly magical power is attached to those short syllables, as if they contained the solution of all problems. Reason and arguments are incapable of combating them… The images evoked by the words, being independent of their meanings, vary from age to age and from people to people, but the formulas remain identical… The Word is merely as it were the button of an electric bell that calls them up."[43]

THE MEETINGS AND PARADES

"The spectacle," says Mucchielli, "is an essential element of the propaganda."

> As for Hitler, he knew admirably how to stage gigantic demonstrations in a style that was both religious and sporting. He spoke from the top of a locomotive or from a giant stand, his metallic platform illuminated by projectors; there were torches, flames, lights in the night, all things that touch the deepest part of human mythology... Hitler borrowed heavily from the practices of the Church where many stimuli create a special state of emotional receptivity. He himself employed light effects of various colors during his speeches by playing a board of electric switches placed on his lectern at the podium. [44]

The spectacle serves many functions. It feeds the need of the masses for "collective communion;" it feels religious. It validates the propaganda by creating a multiplied echo among audience members. Massive audience size, or the impression of massive audience size, feeds the sense of power for the group members. "The impression of mass," says Mucchielli, provides, at the irrational level, the sense of power and force. "For those who are 'inside,' the effect is a boost; for those who are 'outside' (the hesitant, the uncertain) the effect is subjugation by the fascination of force."[45]

He also describes the environment of these events and

rallies as creating "a psychological state of emotional tension which makes the individuals particularly permeable to the propaganda." In psychological terms they create "emotional contagion," and "loss of reflexive control."[46]

Mucchielli's elements of a successful rally will seem familiar. He suggests placing "militants" in the audience, similar to those in the 2015-2016 rallies who beat up hecklers in the audience (who had also likely been planted beforehand). He speaks of "sea of armbands," which has now been translated into a sea of red hats. Aggressive chants, he says, like "Lock her up!", "Build that Wall," or the most current "Fight! Fight! Fight!" act on the crowd, according to Mucchielli, like an electric shock, making them more permeable to propaganda.

Assuming these elements are in place and working, at this point, the characteristics of "blind submission, fierce intolerance, and the need of violent propaganda" will begin to reveal themselves in the psychological behavior of the crowd. The leader is now on his or her way to being acclaimed as a veritable god; what Freud would have called the object for the Eros drive rising simultaneously with the aggressive instincts.

Now that you have lit the fire, what do you do with the heat? And how do you ensure that, as in the case of Mussolini, it doesn't ultimately get directed at you? Enter the scapegoat.

Chapter 4
THE FUNCTION OF THE SCAPEGOAT

You've heard the term. There may have even been one in your school, the kid who got in trouble for things the other kids did. When an underling is punished or convicted of a crime conceived by his superiors, rightly or wrongly, he or she claims to have been made the scapegoat. But the real scapegoat is not quite what you think.

The term goes back to the Book of Leviticus in the Bible, and possibly before. It takes two goats to cleanse a village of its sins. One is sacrificed. The other is released into the wilderness, after the village chief has given it the sins and impurities of the community to take with it. Today it's no longer a goat, it's a person or group. But the scapegoat still wears the sins of others on his or her head—for no other reason than having been chosen to wear them.

A poem by 14th century poet Guillame de Machaut speaks of communities facing the spread of a mysterious disease (presumably the Black Death). The villagers concluded that the Jews must have poisoned the rivers that provide the drinking water. So they massacred them. Afterward, they sang and danced in the streets. Of course, the disease continued killing people after the massacres, in even greater numbers. But for a moment, the villagers had felt better.[47]

The development of the scapegoat in modern propaganda follows the same arc as the other techniques we've seen. In the early decades of the 20th century, as the wave of Freud was still washing over Western and Russian culture, the scapegoat mechanism was one of the group behaviors being cataloged and theorized about. And like the other studies on group behavior, by the 1930s it had become a tool for mass manipulation.

French sociologist Paul Fauconnet was the first to bring it up and "catalog" the phenomenon as a group behavior, in his 1920 thesis *Responsibility*. When there is widespread belief or perception that a society has been damaged, he said, and the collective emotion is fired up, the whole social group is relieved and calmed down by killing the person or thing deemed responsible.[48]

Whether the scapegoat is guilty or innocent is beside the point. It is not a matter of group justice. It is an outlet of group emotion, of collective anger and fear, directed toward a sacrificial victim designated by the leader. The reaction, he says, is "at the same time primitive and collective."

To be effective, the scapegoat must be somebody the community can unite against. They must be able to be destroyed or expelled without creating a new crisis. It should be someone relatively isolated, who no one in the community will stand up to defend. The Jews, who traditionally have lived in their own communities with different traditions than their Christian neighbors, have fit the bill more than once. Immigrants, even those who have lived in the country for hundreds of years, as the Rohingya in Myanmar had, are also a fit.

Mucchielli points out that, for the scapegoat mechanism to work, it is crucial that the process be unconscious. The victim can never be recognized as an innocent scapegoat; he or she must be thought of as a monstrous creature that transgressed some prohibition and deserves to be punished or eliminated. This is the job, of course, of a skilled propagandist, who must engender enough fear and loathing that the audience shudders at the idea of communicating with members of the scapegoat group, where they might find not monsters at all, but fellow human beings.

THE COLLECTIVE PSYCHOSIS

When the propaganda campaign moves from the Propaganda of Indoctrination to the second phase, the Propaganda of Agitation, the scapegoat is the first target for violence. Mucchielli describes how the militants, "hammered by an omnipresent repetition of slogans and by one-dimensional information from media loyal to the propagandist," and "under tension by the propaganda and hate campaigns," enter into a kind of collective psychosis, a collective paranoia, believing they are facing an "enormous machination of traitors to the country, to the cause or the party, a permanent conspiracy."[49]

When triggered, what follows is "a frenzy of unmasking, of suspicion, of denunciation. The certainty builds that the evil is operating by slow and hidden maneuvers, or that a deadly encirclement, a strangulation, is being prepared. The collective psychosis becomes, in the hands of the leaders, a general will to war against the enemy, a will toward the complete removal, the 'radical solution."

Parading the defeated enemy in public or in media, with photos, films, walking of chained prisoners, etc. feeds the psychosis, demonstrates the "concrete" existence of the conspiracy and the danger, and displays the vulnerability and weakness of the opposition in the face of the omnipotent leader and his supporters.

While the scapegoat is the mechanism used to agitate the violence, once unleashed, the violence is rarely limited to them. The Jews were overwhelmingly the central target of the Third Reich's genocide. But even before the camps were erected, while the propaganda was screaming "Jews," other individuals and groups were sent to concentration camps and forced labor camps to die from starvation, disease and brutality. They included communists, socialists, trade unionists, common criminals, Roma (Gypsies), Jehovah's Witnesses, and homosexuals.[50]

Once the violence has started, the scapegoats can be expanded to include anyone who may get in the way. In Nazi Germany "anyone who helped a Jew would be treated as a Jew." In Rwanda moderate Hutus were targeted alongside the Tutsis. Today in Myanmar, Catholic villages and those of other ethnic minorities have been raided, burned, and citizens killed. The scapegoat is the mechanism for the unleashing. Once the violence is unleashed, many old accounts can be settled.

Chapter 5
GROUPS AND OPINION LEADERS

There's an irony in the fact that Propaganda of Indoctrination and the next phase, the Propaganda of Agitation, require freedoms to work, particularly freedom of speech and freedom of the press, even when the end objective is a government where these rights will be eradicated. Under an autocratic regime, ridicule and denigration of the leaders, or accusations and agitation toward violence against the regime, would be swiftly shut down, the instigators carted off to jail and silenced. But in countries where democratic rights are protected, that protection provides the oxygen for the propagandist to broadcast his or her messages. Enemies of our rights and freedoms use our rights and freedoms to take them away from us.

If you are going to conduct a propaganda campaign

to collapse a democratic government and/or install a new regime, the fact that your opponents also have the freedom to counter your words, images, slogans, even your rallies, with their own, becomes a problem. And what is going to prevent readers, listeners, and social media users from simply switching over and listening to, and even seeing the logic of, the other side? Something else is needed to keep the attention of the target audiences fixed on the propagandist's news feed, to cultivate intense antagonism toward any media that may criticize or attempt to engage their audience, to keep them coming back to the right trough—and no other—for more.

The "something else" is the cultivation of groups. It is not about forming new groups or parties and building their membership numbers. It is bringing groups that your target audience members already belong to on board. Getting key voices within these groups repeating and validating your messages gives them credence and reality. Even better, they will couch your message in terms the audience already understands, in words they are already using, from people they already know and trust.

This gives us two more vital tools of the propagandist: cultivation of opinion leaders, and infiltration of groups.

ACTION ON OPINION LEADERS

Opinion leaders are not necessarily the heads of the groups you want to control. They are the people in a community or group your audience is listening to. They are the ones people look to for news and opinions. They act as interpreters, essentially, telling their audiences, in familiar terms, how to view the news, and what it "really means."

The local union representative may be a much stronger opinion leader than the union bosses. In small towns the local sheriff holds far more sway than the Governor who sits far away in the ivory towers of the Capitol building.

Mucchielli puts Opinion Leaders in four main categories:

1. Those who hold social prestige so serve as references or models in the community.

2. Popular people. Psychologists and sociologists use something called a sociogram, which is a graphic representation of the social and interpersonal links each person in a group has. The popular ones emerge as stars in these maps. Mucchielli calls them the "centers of collection and diffusion of unofficial information."

3. The initiators; those who are the first to find out about and try new things. The community pays attention to them, talks about what they are doing, defends their actions, and values their results.

4. The ones we identify with, the people in whom we recognize ourselves, of whom we say "people like you and me." They may be a prominent voice in our age group, our income level, our common interests.

Identifying and investing in the opinion leaders, personally contacting them and persuading them is a great way to increase the numbers when you are trying to penetrate a community. And there's a method to it.

The first phase, prospecting, is done by

sampling people in the target environment, and using, in casual conversations, questions that will allow the infiltrator or infiltrators to identify the group's opinion leaders...They will then go to these people, enter their circle of relations, and develop their persuasion offensive (the charm offensive). They can also enter the target group first, and once they are participants, analyze its structure to discover the opinion leaders. From there, they can efficiently spread 'objective' information that will shape the opinions of people in these groups.[51]

Groups are easily agitated by the exploitation of discontent. "In each social group, the agitator must be able to speak to his listeners about their group interests, their disappointed aspirations, their demands. For this, they must know them and speak in the language of the group. To penetrate the various circles, the organizers of the propaganda of agitation must know their target group's mentality, their stereotypes, their vital concerns, the kind of misery or frustration they endure." You study them. Then you dress, talk, and act to fit in.

COMPROMISING RELIGIONS

Churches historically make useful allies to autocrats and would-be autocrats. Local priests and ministers are among the strongest and most useful opinion leaders. It is the local minister's voice—far more than the actual Church leaders, who may even be overseas—that the parishioners know and hear on a regular basis. In many cases their congregations come every week to hear them. They may know their pastor's wife and children. They may attend pancake breakfasts together.

The local religious leader has the power to interpret the holy scriptures to his or her congregation. Many consider their ministers inspired by powers larger than themselves, powers they can only view with awe. As an Evangelical Christian friend who got married at the suggestion of her pastor once told me, "When the pastor says do it, you DO it." So who would be a more likely authority to interpret the news and events to his or her followers?

Catholic priests and nuns were tried in the International Criminal Court for supporting the massacres of the Tutsis in Rwanda. Buddhist leaders in Myanmar were the primary channels of hate and violence being propagated against the Muslim Rohingya. Patriarch Krill of the Russian Orthodox Church has referred to Putin as a "miracle of God," claimed that the conquest of Ukraine is "God's truth," and promised that Russians who die in Ukraine will go to heaven.

Yes, they often violate some of the most fundamental teachings of their religions in doing so. This is justified by what the group thinks it stands to gain. As priests, pastors, and preachers lend validity and credence to the autocrat's propaganda, they are often led to believe that by doing so they will gain a position of influence in the new regime, have access to the leaders, and the opportunity to legislate their religious agenda or expand their Church's territory and wealth. Should Russia be successful in its conquest of Ukraine, the Ukrainian Orthodox Church would be absorbed by the Russian Orthodox Church, expanding its wealth and territory by 30%.

In the United States, Evangelical pastors and leaders have repeatedly spoken of Donald Trump as being ordained by God to lead the United States, sent as a gift from God, and even by some, as the second coming of Christ. Pentecostal megachurch pastor Paula White, who was installed as the "spiritual advisor" in Trump's White House, was seen on video during his 2020 re-election campaign speaking in tongues and calling on biblical angels to defeat the "high level demonic networks" trying to rig the election, and to ensure Donald Trump's political victory. Why? Speaking before a coalition of 70 Evangelical Christian leaders who advised the 2016 Trump presidential campaign and the Trump White House on religious matters, White claimed that "Our unity brought unprecedented victories, influence and access."

In May, 2022, right-wing Pastor Greg Locke, who has 1.8 million followers on Facebook, shouted from the pulpit that he did not want Democrats in his Church. He is not alone, though his language is more colorful than most. "If you're a Democrat," he said, "Get out, you demon. You get out, you baby-butchering election thief. You cannot be a Christian and vote Democrat in this nation. They are God-denying demons that hate this nation." As the murmurs of the congregation turn to cheers, Locke said "Everyone talks about the insurrection. Let me tell you something. You ain't seen the insurrection yet. You keep pushing our buttons, you low-down, sorry compromisers, you God-hating communists, you'll find out what an insurrection is." The audience broke into applause.

The Evangelical Christian coalition behind the Trump campaign did not just "come together." Like the Buddhist support of the military regime in Myanmar, it was orchestrated and well executed, and continues to be built and agitated, by an adept and well-trained propagandist. When the history of the period is studied, and people involved speak out, we will know more.

SUBVERSION: SETTING THE STAGE FOR OVERTHROW

Not all groups are to be allied. Some have to be gotten rid of. With these, Mucchielli says, subversive agents will "have to enter them, with the sole purpose of disassociating them." This destruction from within is accomplished by inciting the "enemy population (or one of its factions)" to act against its own leadership.

The history and psychological warfare techniques of subversion are so extensive that Mucchielli has relegated them to a separate booklet. Much of what he says is drawn from the communist revolutions around the world, where subversion of groups and institutions was a critical factor in bringing on the collapse of existing governments. But to outline:

Mucchielli says there are two essential levers for subversion: small groups and mass media. Small groups, he says, "use a kind of jiu jitsu policy," which allows a small, light fighter to easily overcome a larger and stronger opponent. The idea is that very small and mobile groups can use the natural inertia of the large group, a colonial authority for example, to "tip them over."

On a larger scale, when one wants to subvert an entire state, the first action is the "neutralization of the use of popular consultation." The vote. "One of the astonishing modern revolutionary messages to come from parties and groups that have always apparently fought for universal suffrage and democracy, has been that elections equal betrayal."

Writing in 1970, Mucchielli could not have foreseen what happened 50 years later after a democratic election in the United States. Instead, he pulls examples from revolutionary groups in Latin America, including the Peruvian revolutionaries who proclaimed in July 1966 that as a "genuine revolutionary movement," they had "pushed back the paths of compromise and agreement with the exploiters... and discarded the bourgeois method of elections." In Venezuela in 1962, the "Revolutionary Front" denounced what they called electoral farce and fought to make elections impossible.

Today we have better examples, including fabrications of Venezuelans and Italians rigging American voting machines, accusing the voting equipment manufacturers of being in on the "steal," non-existent "vote dumps" in the middle of the night, and election workers running covert operations to swing the US presidency to Joe Biden.

Similar claims were used by the generals of Myanmar's Tatmadaw when they seized power in the military coup in 2021 (and this is a good time to remind you that the generals trained on propaganda in Moscow); they publicly justified it by claiming that massive voter fraud had been uncovered in the previous year's election and "was threatening the future of the country." The junta's Buddhist supporters filled the streets carrying banners echoing the claims.

The former President of Brazil, Jair Bolsonaro, spent years undermining confidence in Brazil's elections, claiming in 2018 that hackers had tried and failed to steal 12 million votes from him. His charges were found to be false by election officials and fact-checkers. Yet he consistently and methodically repeated them and other baseless claims about Brazil's voting system, in speeches, interviews, and hundreds of posts on social media. By August, 2021, two months before he faced popular democrat President Luiz Inacio Lula da Silva (Lula) in a new election, a poll showed that three out of four of Bolsonaro's supporters had little or no faith in Brazil's election machines. When he was defeated, Bolsonaro's supporters camped in front of the military barracks demanding a military coup to save the country. In January, 2023, taking a cue from the Americans, a mob of his supporters attacked Brazil's federal government buildings in the nation's capital, Brasilia.

There is a reason why elections are a first target, aside from the obvious one, that if one cannot take a country by vote it can be used to agitate one's followers to take it by force. But with distrust in elections well sowed, Mucchielli says. "Revolutionary action can thereafter only be carried out by a minority, by a small group or groups." And the small nucleus can claim to be acting for "the people." In other words, majority rule is gone; democracy is dead.

From there, "key" groups are selected to be brought down.

THE ACTION PLAN

A person's social groups—particularly those defined by psychologists as "primary" groups—act as bulwarks against propaganda for their members. Those that do not move in step with the propaganda can become places where people can discuss events and exchange ideas. They provide openings for people to doubt what they may have heard, thus weakening the positions of the propagandist.

These groups can include non-allied Churches, college associations, groups formed around social causes, etc. Until these groups are demoralized and "disassociated," propaganda can fail; the group members may listen to each other more closely than they do to the propagandist. The shared loyalty to the group's core of opinions, norms, and values make them resistant to attack from the outside. As long as they remain primary groups for members of society, "the totalitarian grip of the conscience becomes impossible."

"Subversive agents," Mucchielli says, "will therefore have to enter the groups with the sole purpose of disassociating them. The operations will be carried out by a subversive agent who has previously penetrated the group through normal channels and has been a "member" long enough to be well regarded. If this maneuver is impossible, a relay will have to be found among the well-established members of the group."

Once the agent, or agents, are in place, they follow a plan that centers on weakening the bonds of the group and unraveling the goodwill and loyalty of its members. The tactics of this plan are to:

1. Create doubt. Question the certainties of the group by appearing to be "worried" and searching for truth.

2. Bring "information" to the group that is problematic and provokes internal discussion and uncertainty.

3. Discredit the group leaders when they try to reunite the group. Inject distrust through rumors or subversive attacks. Use *ad hominem* attacks, i.e. attacks on the character, if necessary;

4. Use "free, democratic, discussion" during meetings to manipulate individual opinions by group pressure, or, failing that, to confuse members of the group.

5. Simultaneously maintain excellent public relations so as not to be attacked personally by the group.

When the subversives are in the group "like a fish in water," they will know the group members' habits, their mentality, their needs. Now they apply "special techniques":

1. Represent oneself and fellow members of the small subversive group as the exclusive defenders of the interests of the larger group. To the extent this is done well they will attract "good souls, supporters, and a general complicity."

2. The "Provocation-Repression-Call for Unity of Action Against Repression." The aim is to "organize a spectacular action" by the small group against the power, in the name of the interests of the group. It should be made clear

to the "ordinary" group members that this is being done for their benefit or protection. The action must be one that is sure to provoke a reaction of repression from the power, so one can then paint oneself as the victim of that repression. This is usually enough to appeal to the group for solidarity and to lead an average or even large group of supporters in a counter-reaction. Be egging on the group members to additional "reprimandable" or provocative actions, creating more repression by the leaders, the process to begin to snowball.

3. Release the actions and the resulting "repression" to the mass media, ensuring that it is presented with your spin and significance. If the action is sufficiently spectacular, the media will send special envoys to interview the revolutionary leaders, bringing back speeches, recordings, films, articles, photos, etc.

4. Stage demonstrations of "solidarity" at different locations that are also well covered by the media. The powers of the group at this point would discredit themselves if they try to stop them.

5. Continue the escalation by carrying out increasingly unbearable provocations until the expected effect is obtained and the process is set in motion again.

If the subversive is able to damage key positions, the "traffic jam" and paralysis spreads rapidly. If key positions in the group are occupied, or destroyed by the subversives, the whole machine, i.e. the whole group, can be stopped.

If effectively subverted, the targeted group (or state) will eventually collapse on its own. The leaders and those who have tried to oppose the subversive agents will go away by themselves. "They will leave on their own, under the indifferent eye of the population, through the effect of the decay of all authority."

The strength of the subversives, Mucchielli says, is that they can so easily operate undetected. Discontent "happens." Anger flares. People leave. Groups collapse or just dissipate. You see the puppet play but you never see the strings, even when they are right in front of you, because you aren't looking for them. "The man in the street, the average citizen, ignores the existence of subversion and 'does not believe it.' Those who have heard of it, or suspect it, expect it to stand out to view or assume that only the fringe elements are permeable to it."

Governments, he says, minimize it because they have confidence in the stability and the enormity of the masses, believing that they will be "hard to get moving" if the economic conditions of revolution—economic disparity, injustice, mass unemployment, etc.—are not met. They have not realized, as Mucchielli did, that in the absence of the economic conditions, the psychological methods work just as well.

Chapter 6
PHASE 2: THE PROPAGANDA OF AGITATION

"With a minimum of technique, one can launch (and all the warlike speeches are so many illustrations) groups, masses, peoples, in the massacre of other groups or other peoples, with the good conscience of being the legitimate defense and the militants of the Supreme Good." —Roger Mucchielli

By now, if the Propaganda of Indoctrination and Recruitment was done well, the audience will be looking at the world through the propagandist's filters. They will explain the global situation to themselves and each other using the worldview they have been fed. They hate the people the leader wants them to hate. They adore and feel empowered by the leader and his or her spokespeople. They are ready to stand by their leader's side to nobly save the nation. They may have even stashed weapons to do so.

Everything done so far has been preparing the ground for this point, the point where the fire is lit and ignites the aggression. This is the start of the overthrow.

Acting aggressively is not normal every-day behavior for most of us. Yes, it is a fundamental animal and human instinct—what Mucchielli calls "a sudden explosion of the will to survive"—that is extremely useful if your herd or your beehive is being threatened. But we no longer have saber-toothed tigers threatening our loved ones or warring tribes coming over the hill. Today, the kind of blind violence Mucchielli is referring to, including torture and atrocities, needs a perceived or imagined threat to trigger it. It needs to be enough of a threat that you must act against it—at the leader's direction.

One of the problems today with trying to incite mobs to violence is that there are government structures in place that are meant to reduce armed conflict, and where implemented they have been successful. The Age of Reason, the era that produced Thomas Jefferson, natural rights, and American democracy, was a major advancement of civilization founded on the assumption that we are far more than animals whose behavior is dictated by primal instincts, that we are capable of using dialog, argument and common interests instead of violence and war to settle our differences. The sword and the gun were to be replaced by the negotiating table and the ballot box. Imperfect, yes (particularly if you were a woman or Black at the time). But where democracy has flourished, war has receded.

After World War II, 27 countries, including Germany, Italy, Austria, and Japan, transitioned to a form of democratic government, and remain so today. The United Nations, imperfect as it is, was formed to bring conflict and argument to a new global platform, as an alternative to arms. The world did not become perfect, by far. And the UN has its own set of problems. But the fact remains that since it was formed, to date there has not been another world war. The soil of France, Germany, England, once soaked in the blood of their young men through endless wars, has not seen another war.

For some, this is not good enough. It does not satisfy their lust for power or immeasurable wealth. Instead of compromise and finding shared interests with their fellow humans who have different cultures, values, and politics, they set about to rule over them or destroy them. As we do not live in the threatening environments of the past, achieving that destruction requires painting the reality of a growing threat around the members of the "herd," relighting the old herd instincts and the drives to kill or destroy intruders by portraying them as invaders or infiltrators attempting to breach our territory and creating the threat that they will destroy all that the members hold dear.

When the agitation is done correctly, the barriers against harming those outsiders will have started to crumble as aggression comes to the forefront. The members of the group will be starting to feel like the warring tribes will be storming the gates any minute now. Or, worse, that they could already be in our midst, preparing to destroy us. Now it is primarily a matter of playing on emotions repeatedly and with increasing intensity—anger and indignation, hatred, resentment, exasperation—and linking these to situations of frustration and damage suffered. Then, with sufficient drama, pointing the way to eliminate the supposed threat.

The Propaganda of Agitation doesn't work on everyone. Many, even those whose views and beliefs align with the "new leader," will have families, groups, education, that act as bulwarks against being agitated to violence. But it doesn't need to work on everyone. It only needs to work on enough. As we saw with Hitler's Brown Shirts, and Russia's Bolsheviks, small violent groups can plunge an entire society into chaos. The rest will be dealt with in Phase 3, the Propaganda of Integration, after the violence has done its job and the system has collapsed.

Of course, it takes more than speaking to a group about the destructive forces coming over the hill. The strength, theatrical ability, and charisma of the speaker—as you can see if you watch the public speeches of Mussolini, Hitler, Trump, and others—have as much to do with the audience reaction as the buttons they are pushing. Mucchielli stresses that the speaker or agitator must be able to "speak to people in the language they understand, to insinuate oneself into their desires and resentments, to evoke their values in order to mobilize their motivations." But through it all you will hear the message that "you have been the victim, you have suffered at their hands, you have been humiliated by those bastards who are trying to destroy your country. We are strong enough to get rid of them together, and when we do, we will walk together into a new day."

All communication in this phase is intended to orient the listener and lead them to the expected action. The agitator provides the significance to events. No explanation, or even understanding, is needed. Even truthfulness is irrelevant. This is not a matter of engaging reason.

THE WATCHWORD

Pay attention to the slogans. As covered earlier, in Phase 1, the Propaganda of Indoctrination and Recruitment, the slogan answers the motivations and aspirations of the audience. The first Nazi slogan was "Ein volk, Ein Reich, Ein Führer" ("One people, one empire, one Führer"). Another slogan, directed to workers, promised "Work and Bread." The first Bolshevik slogan was "Peace, Land, and Bread." Donald Trump's "Make America Great Again" sets a similar tone here in our own country.

When the propaganda phase shifts from indoctrination to agitation, the slogan becomes a call to action, a call for the hammer to come down. As Mucchielli describes it, "the watchword is the striking formula of the short-term action to be undertaken, or of the immediate results to be obtained."

The slogan calling the followers to the Capitol on January 6 was "Stop the Steal." The first slogan of Donald Trump's 2024 campaign was "Save America." These do not reflect aspirations. They are calls to action, signaling the shift from Phase 1 to Phase 2.

THE LANGUAGE CHANGES

At this point, keeping in mind that one of the goals of Phase 1 was to disengage reason, in this second phase your propaganda becomes simplified to speak to the "mind" that is now engaged, what Mucchielli refers to as the primitive or unconscious mind, that can be triggered to violence.

This is not a mind that thinks or speaks in logic. The primitive mind, he says, is a system that is based on absolutes and opposing symbols. It is far more binary—us and them, good and evil, light and dark. To bring it to life and bring it into action, you speak to it in its own language:

> In all propaganda, in order to be able to reach the most elementary levels of comprehension and to use a very deep archaic scheme in humans (day and night becoming symbols of life and death, light and darkness, truth and lie, good and evil), there is a hyper-simplification of data and causes, doctrines and intentions... 'He who is not with us is against us.' There are only two sides: us and the others. All the others are 'objectively complicit'. We are your life, the way, the truth, the light; they are therefore death, the impasse, the lie, the darkness.
>
> So the propagandist will fight the evil in the name of the good. The struggle encompasses all forms of warfare; all will be a legitimate defense... The mechanism will lead him to unleash an unrestrained violence since this one is exercised in the name of the Good, therefore of the Morality ...The Nazis 'purging the world of Jewish vermin,' the McCarthyites chasing the communist ideology in the USA, the communist regimes chasing the plotters against the people...and all the fanatics of the world...are convinced that they are working for the common good. This makes them perfectly guilt-free.[52]

Or put another way:

> The final action demanded, that is, murder, always appears in the capsule of values and legitimacy...Our cause is the just cause, it is the cause of humanity. Whoever fights for this cause sacrifices himself to humanity and its progress. He who fights against this cause is, therefore, a war criminal (or a servant of Satan, according to the times). He puts himself in the ban of humanity and must be crushed like vermin or hanged like a criminal.[53]

Long-time advisor to Donald Trump, Roger Stone, is apparently well versed in most of the techniques Mucchielli describes. For example, on the evening of January 5, 2021, as the crowd was being warmed up for the storming of the US Capital the next day, Stone (who had been convicted and jailed in 2019 for obstruction of justice, making false statements, and witness tampering during the Congressional investigation of Russian meddling in the 2016 elections, and was later pardoned by Trump), stepped on stage to address the crowd in one of his signature pinstriped suits and a feathered fedora, a dance track blasting behind him. "This is nothing less than an epic struggle for the future of this country," he shouted. "It's between dark and light. Between the Godly and the Godless. Between good and evil. And we will win this fight or America will step off into a thousand years of darkness. We dare not fail."

Since April, 2021, Stone and Michael Flynn (who twice pled guilty to making false statements to federal investigators regarding his Russian connections, and who like Stone, was pardoned by Trump) have been barnstorming the United States with their "ReAwaken America" campaign, aimed at Evangelical Christians. They are at times joined by MyPillow CEO Mike Lindell or Eric Trump. Attendees are told that "We're under spiritual warfare" and "They hate you because they hate Jesus," that it is time to "put on the whole armor of God." Then Michael Flynn invites the audience to be baptized.

In May 2021, Flynn also spoke at the Omni Hotel in Dallas, at a QAnon rally entitled "For God and Country Patriot Roundup." The military coup in Myanmar had happened only three months before. QAnon supporters had been celebrating the coup online and saying the US military should take similar action against President Biden, the illegitimate President.

Flynn was asked by someone in the audience "why can't what happened in Myanmar happen here." Flynn's response: "No reason. It could happen here. I mean, it should happen here." The audience cheered exuberantly.

At a ReAwaken rally in Myrtle Beach, South Carolina, Roger Stone announced that "There is a satanic portal above the White House, you can see it day and night. It exists. It is real. And it must be closed." The "portal," Stone said, first appeared after Joe Biden "became president and it will be closed before he leaves."

At another, in the Amish Country of Pennsylvania in November 2022, speaker and self-declared prophet Julie Green told the audience God had spoken to her and sent a prophecy. "These are the days for you to control the governments of this earth," she said to enthusiastic applause. "God said he can take this country back in unconventional ways. He doesn't need an election to do it." Green had previously claimed that Joe Biden was dead and Obama was controlling his body double, and that God had told her that Prince Charles would murder the Queen.

Michael Flynn and Roger Stone are talking to an audience they have come to know well, an audience that has been well infiltrated, well indoctrinated, and is now ready to stand by Donald Trump, with arms if necessary, to save their nation from the forces of darkness and the "demons" that threaten their cause, the cause of the Supreme Good. The audience listening to Roger Stone talk about the satanic portal was described as "rapt."

But the language of agitation is not limited to Evangelical Christians. On March 4, 2023, Donald Trump addressed the Conservative Political Action Conference (CPAC) in Maryland with a message that would become a common theme in his social media posts throughout the year. "For seven years," he said, "you and I have been engaged in an epic struggle to rescue our country from the people who hate it and want to absolutely destroy it. The sinister forces trying to kill America have done everything they can to stop me, to silence you, and to turn this nation into a socialist dumping ground for criminals, junkies, Marxists, thugs, radicals, and dangerous refugees…

"This is the final battle. They know it, I know it, you know it, everybody knows it. This is it. Either they win or we win. And if they win, we no longer have a country."

As I am writing, the United States is clearly in the

middle of Phase 2, the Propaganda of Agitation, moving precisely as Mucchielli described the steps. If you listen and watch through the prism that Mucchielli has handed to us, it will be far more clear. When Donald Trump declares that our justice system is broken, that our elections are rigged, our economy is a shambles, and our country is being destroyed by those who broke it, becoming upset that he is lying or calling it disinformation is missing the point. Trump is not speaking to you or me. Your expectation that his communication should be reasonable and honest is the expectation of someone who is unfamiliar with the technique.

There are others running disinformation campaigns for the purpose of swaying elections, in more countries than ours. But the language from Donald Trump, Michael Flynn, Roger Stone, and the others who echo them, is a different category. It is a consistent message, reaching its intended audiences many times a day-- the day is coming when it will be time to save the nation from destruction at the hands of the Left. If it is not done by legitimate election, the system is so badly broken, and the Left so intent on destroying the nation, that it will have to be by taking up arms. By doing so, you will be patriots saving the nation.

It is worth saying again that the Indonesians who killed hundreds of thousands of their countrymen in 1965-66 believed they were being patriots and saving their nation. The Rwandan Hutus taking machetes and hoes to their Tutsi neighbors believed they were being patriots and saving their nation from a threat that would destroy it. The Buddhists of Myanmar when they attacked and killed, raped, and burned the villages of the Muslim Rohingya, believed they were patriots saving their nation from a threat that would destroy their nation and religion.

Will Americans slide into injuring and harming our neighbors? Of course I would like to think not. Like you, I have grown up in an America of peace, and civilization, as imperfect as it has been. I want to believe we are better than that, that Christians will realize when their pastor tells them to "slay the Democrat demons" that he or she is going against the most basic teachings of Christ, and that we can find other ways to overcome our differences. But we would be fools to miss the fact that the same techniques are being used on our own countrymen and women, to ignite the same fire in Americans that was lit in the Germans, Indonesians, Rwandans, and Myanmar Buddhists. Whatever the final result of the agitation taking place, it is intended to shatter the sense of civility to our neighbors we have come to expect in our neighborhoods and communities.

Chapter 7
PHASE 3: THE PROPAGANDA OF INTEGRATION

The propaganda of integration comes after the overthrow, and after the installation of the new regime; it is about holding onto the power once it has been seized. It "brings the outliers into the fold, by force if necessary." This is accomplished by completely reshaping the opinions, attitudes, and behaviors in the population.

The principles of integration, Mucchielli says, can apply in a nation that has just come under a dictatorship or military regime. It can also be applied inside an ideological group (including, perhaps, a political party) by new leaders, to obtain the "total commitment" of the group

The goals of this phase include:

1. Unanimity, or consensus. Complete agreement among the group or population. Leaders cannot tolerate

independence in any form.

2. Conformity. It is not just a matter of imposing or gaining consensus on the objectives on the group. Group members or citizens must be made active participants in achieving the group's objectives.

3. The radical change of opinions and behavior as dictated by the new regime, which Mucchielli likens to mass religious conversion. This may involve a reinterpretation of facts, of events, of history—and even of the individual's own past, if needed. Old heroes may have to be written out of the story.

4. Correct action. One doesn't only demonstrate their loyalty with words. The new regime requires a commitment to action. This can range from participation in rallies and waving flags to turning in those harboring Jews if you are in Nazi Germany, reporting on and denouncing your neighbors if you are in the Soviet Union. Legislators are expected to pass the right laws, courts to return the right verdicts, at the risk of being labeled traitors.

If this is going to work, he cautions, it must be no less than 100% in every aspect. Getting there, however, can get ugly:

> Let us emphasize the need for propaganda of this kind to go all the way in each of its initiatives. One of the most serious factors of failure is half-measures.... Every technique must be totalitarian, or it will be ineffective; it is this internal requirement that makes both the inhumanity and the fundamental fragility of these processes.

In an ideological integration program, the malcontents are dangerous. The dictator cannot tolerate them, because they are potential opponents. Certainly, there are the 'administrative liquidations,' the suicides, deportation, concentration camps. [54]

THE NEW ROLE OF THE SCAPEGOAT

In the propaganda of integration, the scapegoat returns, but in a different form. Now the target is the sinister forces within. In Phase 1 and 2 the scapegoat is a distinct and "different" group (immigrants, Muslims, Jews). In Phase 3 they sit among us. It could be the man or woman next to you in Church, a military leader or member of Congress who could be secretly working against the group.

Say you've promised a new world by destroying the old. What do you do when the new one doesn't materialize? When your indoctrinated, chanting, symbol-flying, ready-to-beat-someone-up followers don't see the promised change? Sooner or later, what Mucchielli calls the gap between the "myths of historical proclamations and the miserable reality" becomes obvious; when it does, malcontents within the movement will start to rear their heads.

If you are the leader or the ruling group, there is a risk that one of those malcontents will be charismatic. People may start to listen to him or her. He or she could even start to direct the action of people within your movement. With the fire of reactionary aggressiveness already lit, a development like this could lead to an explosion of violence that you might not be able to control. As Mussolini learned, the goal of the group could even become getting you.

A dictator's answer is fairly straightforward. The critics and malcontents may mysteriously commit suicide or fall from a window. They may suddenly die of an unknown cause in prison. There are camps they can be sent to. The party may need a purge.

For those lacking the ability to simply "disappear" the unrest, the malcontents can be labeled and publicly exposed as "infiltrators" for the enemy. They become the Phase 3 form of scapegoat—traitors to the cause.

Mucchielli points out the multiple advantages of the "enemy within" scapegoat:

• They divert anger, and serve as an outlet for the group's emotion, while channeling it away from the leaders.

• They divert the attention of the members of the group who could otherwise start to analyze the internal causes of the failures.

• They serve as an explanation of the failures of the group and the dissatisfaction of its members.

• The "enemy within" scapegoat allows the development of police terror; a police state becomes necessary to "assure the security and peace of the group." The authorities must hunt down traitors for the continued survival of the group.

• It intensifies the cohesion of the group by using the group reflex of survival in the face of an enemy or in the face of danger.

• It keeps the group under emotional tension, which

is a state of suggestibility very favorable to the injection of propaganda slogans and to the credibility of official information.

Even more than in Phase 1, the scapegoat cannot be created with rallies or lectures or even writings. The enemy within and their intent to destroy the group must be felt viscerally, with the "traitors" hunted down (perhaps reported on), unmasked, and paraded publicly in defeat before being silenced:

> It is very important, therefore, that this figure of the 'Enemy' is not an abstraction or a simple story. It is very important to bring proof, to organize the spectacular demonstration of its existence. Hence the publicity given to certain 'documents,' to certain 'confessions,' to certain 'captures'; faces will be shown, treachery will be made palpable and perceptible.[55]

THE UNITED STATES

Accomplishing the goals of integration on a national scale requires the spilling of blood. Voices must be permanently silenced, whether they disappear, are shipped off to camps as enemies of the state, or are executed after a "military tribunal" for treason. Because the United States and other democracies are at the moment protected by their constitutions and the courts, it is easy to dismiss as "not what's happening here."

It is easier to envision in an ideological group, church,

movement, or political party; they can create uniformity by the expulsion and banning of those who refuse to conform to their thinking. The leaders can virtually remove the old guard and erase the old heroes from the group's history.

Donald Trump and his speechwriters have achieved a purge of the Republican party, not with trials and executions, but with mockery, derision, and expulsion. By coining the term RINO (Republican in Name Only) and launching scathing personal attacks against Republican leaders who have criticized the new leader or failed to fall in line with the extremists in Congress, he has effectively banished the former leaders from the party and has effectively written them out of the party's history. In many cases he has turned them into laughingstocks among the loyalists of the new party. Those "gone" from the conversation include former President George W. Bush, former Speakers of the House Paul Ryan and John Boehner, former Presidential candidate Mitt Romney, former Naval officer, lion of the Senate and Presidential candidate John McCain. And the list goes on.

Mitch McConnell, a US Senator for 38 years, is the top Republican in Congress. Since 2003 he has served as majority whip, Senator Majority Leader, and Senate Minority Leader; he is the longest-serving party leader in Senate history. After issuing some mild rebukes regarding Donald Trump's language, while continuing to vote the Republican party line, and consistently using his position to forward Republican interests, he also ended up on Donald Trump's chopping block. After failing to toe the extremist line in Congress and negotiating with Democrats, Speaker of the

House Kevin McCarthy joined the list of the banished as well, despite having made several trips to Mar-a-Lago to curry Trump's favor.

Liz Cheney, the daughter of a family once considered Republican royalty and a leading ideological conservative, served as the Chair of the House Republican Conference, the third most powerful position in Congress, for three years. After she openly criticized Trump and repeatedly pushed back on Trump's false claims that the 2020 election was "stolen," she was removed as conference chair through a voice vote led by House Speaker Kevin McCarthy. Minutes before the vote, Trump advised the caucus that they had "a great opportunity today to rid themselves of a poor leader, a major Democrat talking point, a warmonger, and a person with absolutely no personality or heart."[56] After serving as vice chair of the committee to investigate the January 6 Capitol insurrection, in 2023 Cheney was challenged in a primary for her seat against Trump-endorsed Harriet Hageman. She lost, with 28.9% of the vote to Hageman's 66.3%.

Today Ronald Reagan's name is rarely heard of except in false quotes implying that he endorsed Donald Trump for President.

I challenge you to find one Republican leader from the last few decades who has not been mocked, discredited, and virtually erased from the history of the Republican party. To the Trump loyalists, history of the Republican party has been rewritten—including the elimination of heroes who were once the pride of the party.

In March 2023, Donald Trump, speaking at a

Conservative Political Action Conference (CPAC) event, crowed about the accomplishment. "When we started this journey," he said, "We had a Republican party that was ruled by freaks, neo-cons, globalists, open border zealots, and fools. But we are never going back to the party of Paul Ryan, Karl Rove, and Jeb Bush." The ovation from the audience was long and thunderous. "We are never going to be a country ruled by entrenched political dynasties in both parties, rotten special interests, China-loving politicians, of which there are many. Are you listening, Mitch McConnell? Are you listening?" Laughter and boos from the audience.

Steps One, Two, and Three of the Propaganda on Integration within the Republican party are complete. The party has been Born Again. Step Four, the forcing of correct action, not just by party members but by judges, governors, and members of Congress, is still underway.

INTEGRATION IN THE 20th CENTURY

There are three clear examples of the Propaganda of Integration on a national scale in the 20th Century—the Soviet Union, Communist China, and Nazi Germany. I'm going to take one slice of these events—Germany from 1932 -1934—to show how Phase 3 was initiated. This is not a comprehensive history; we all know that the story of Nazi Germany gets much, much worse after 1934. It's an illustration of integration after assuming power, the bringing about of a change of heart in those who are not in line, "by force if necessary." (A closer view of the rise of Nazi Germany is brilliantly covered in four books by Richard Evans. I quote one of them, *The Coming of the Third Reich*, frequently here).

THE RISE OF THE BROWNSHIRTS

Before the rise of the Schutzstaffel (SS) and Gestapo, it was the Sturmabteilung, the SA, or Brownshirts, that provided the force needed for Adolph Hitler's rise to power. Its story starts in 1919.

After Germany's defeat in World War I in 1918, German troops were brought home. Their exact numbers are not recorded, but 13 million Germans had served in the military during the war. Depending on what you read, 1.5 million to 2.5 million of these men were killed, 4.2 million were wounded, and more than a million taken prisoner. The Germany they returned to was in upheaval. Kaiser Wilhelm II, the Emperor of Germany and the Commander-in-Chief of the German armed forces, had abdicated his throne and fled to Holland. Before leaving, the Kaiser had handed power to the left-wing Social Democratic Party, led by Friedrich Ebert.

Communist uprisings were further threatening the country's stability. With an army restricted to 100,000 troops by the Treaty of Versailles, the country was ill equipped to restore or maintain order. The German High Command began to encourage individual officers to recruit independent volunteer units, called *Freikorps*.

This network of independent militias proliferated across Germany and in other parts of Europe. The *Freikorps* were initially composed of veterans of the war, some of whom had returned mentally or physically damaged and were not able to reintegrate into civilian society. Humiliated by their defeat in the war, the comradery and heroic spirit of brothers in battle provided by the pseudo-military structure of the militia at home gave them a place to land. They were still at war, though now, with little to no regulation, they were even more unbridled:

> But who were these soldiers and why did they remain in uniform? Their reasons varied. Some had no home to which they could return--or at least felt that way. Others had come to crave the bonding that is unique to men under fire. Some were legitimately unhinged after four years of mud, blood, and bombardment--the unholy trinity of trench warfare. And many were too young to have fought in the war at all, a fact that has generally gone unrecognized in studies of the *Freikorps* --- they were eager to grab a chance for glory.
>
> Politically, a "freebooter" (*Freikorpskämpfer*) was a man of the Right, but he was more than that. He was also a hater. He hated the revolution, hated the new German Republic, hated the Socialists who led it and the Communists trying to replace them. Indeed, he hated civilians in general. He believed that Germany had not lost the war but had been "stabbed in the back" by the same pack of traitors now ruling in Berlin. He might have had a sentimental attachment to the old Germany of the Kaiser, but he was savvy enough to realize that those days were gone forever. While most of

PHASE 3: THE PROPAGANDA OF INTEGRATION

his ideas remained inchoate [not fully formed], he yearned for a powerful Germany united under a strong leader (*Führer*), a political system stamped with the same military virtues of authority and obedience as the army at the front.[57]

The *Freikorps* primarily fought the communists and socialists in German society, extracting revenge from the people they believed were responsible for Germany's defeat.

In January 1919, the Spartacus League, which would become the Communist Party of Germany (KPD), staged an uprising in Berlin. Armed party members seized control of the central city, and declared the Ebert government deposed. The Minister of Defense brought in the *Freikorps*. Robert Citino of *Military History Magazine* eloquently describes what happens next:

> Civil wars are always brutal, but the zeal with which the *Freikorps* went about their business was out of all proportion. They killed during and after battle with equal gusto, and any prisoner unlucky enough to fall into their hands could usually expect a bullet or a gun-butt to the back of the head. Indeed, each and every *Freikorps* man who wrote his memoirs bragged about it in print.
>
> Their most infamous victims were the KPD leaders Karl Liebknecht and Rosa Luxemburg, captured by soldiers of the Guards Cavalry Rifle Division (*Garde-Kavallerie-Schützen-Division*).

Their captors first clubbed them senseless, then shot them for "attempting to escape," perhaps the first use of this characteristic 20th century phrase. Luxemburg was small, physically frail, and suffered from a childhood hip ailment that left one leg longer than the other. It is difficult, to put it mildly, to imagine her trying to escape from a troop of heavily armed soldiers. In classic gangster style, her killers tossed her body into the icy waters of Berlin's Landwehrkanal and dumped Liebknecht's corpse without any identifying information on the steps of a local mortuary.[58]

After a Bolshevik takeover of Bavaria in May 1919, 30,000 *Freikorps* members were sent to the region, assassinating suspected communists and social democrats en masse. By one account, as a result of the *Freikorps*' violence, "Munich's undertakers were overwhelmed, resulting in bodies lying in the streets and decaying until mass graves were completed." [59]

In 1921, as their methods and independence became a threat to the Weimar administration, *Freikorp*s members were culled from the military. The government support they had received, in funding and equipment, was stopped. The *Freikorps* numbers quickly declined. By 1923 the *Freikorps* were more known for street fighting and pub brawls than attacking or assassinating dissident communists.

There was one group that didn't fade. In 1923 the members of the Bavarian *Freikorps* group were used to form the

Sturmabteilung, or SA, the militia attached to the newly formed National Socialist Party, the Nazi party. The SA were assigned to provide military protection for the party while also advancing Nazi ideology. By March 1923, when the WWI fighter plane ace, Hermann Göring, assumed leadership of the SA, it provided Hitler's personal security detail and military support to enforce Hitler's orders, and was given responsibility for preventing the functioning of opposing parties, by whatever means necessary. It was the SA that orchestrated the failed Beer Hall Putsch in November 1923, after which Hitler was arrested and jailed for nine months.

By 1925 the SA had 6000 members. In 1930 Hitler appointed a German military leader, early Nazi party member and close friend, Ernst Röhm, Chief of the SA. By January 1931, it had 221,000 members. As unemployment skyrocketed in Germany, by 1933 the SA membership had soared to millions.

The SA became an integral part of the choreographed spectacle of the Nazi rallies. On January 30, 1933, for the rally in Berlin celebrating Hitler's appointment as chancellor, the SA marched in the streets of Berlin carrying fiery torches, cheered on by thousands of German citizens who had gathered to pay homage to President Paul von Hindenburg and Hitler, who appeared at separate windows over the parade. French Ambassador André François-Poncet, watching from a nearby window, described the torches as they "formed a river of fire...over the very heart of the city. From these brown-shirted, booted men, as they marched in perfect discipline and alignment, their well-pitched voices bawling war-like songs, there rose an enthusiasm and dynamism that were extraordinary." [60]

Melita Maschmann, then a 15-year-old Nazi supporter, watched the parade that evening. As an adult, she recalled, "Some of the uncanny feeling of that night remains with me even today. The crashing treads of booted feet, the somber pomp of the red and black flags, the flickering light from the torches on the faces and the songs with melodies that were at once aggressive and sentimental." [61]

When not on stage, the SA broke up the meetings of opposing political parties, pulling leaders out and beating them viciously, at times to death; they fought in the streets with other paramilitaries, terrorized voters who expressed support for opposition parties, and terrorized Jews, Roma, Communists, and Social Democrats—groups they believed were "enemies of Germany."[62] But they were more than street thugs. And their violence went virtually unchecked. From Richard Evans in *The Coming of the Third Reich*:

> Many of those who attempted to prosecute acts of torture and violence committed by Nazi stormtroopers were themselves fully paid-up Nazis. The Bavarian Justice Minister who tried to prosecute acts of torture in Dachau in 1933, for example, was none other than Hans Frank, later to acquire a brutal reputation as Governor-General of Poland during the Second World War. Nothing came of these legal initiatives, which were all frustrated by intervention from above, by SS leader, Heinrich Himmler, or ultimately, by Hitler himself.

PHASE 3: THE PROPAGANDA OF INTEGRATION

An amnesty for crimes committed in the 'national uprising' was passed as early as 21 March 1933, quashing over 7,000 prosecutions. Everybody, including not least the Nazis, was aware throughout 1933 and 1934 that the brutal beatings, torture, maltreatment, destruction of property and violence of all kinds carried out against the Nazis' opponents, up to and including murder by the brown-shirted stormtroopers of the SA and the black-uniformed squads of the SS, were in flagrant violation of the law of the land. Yet this violence was a central, indispensable part of the Nazi seizure of power from February 1933 onwards, and the widespread, in the end almost universal fear that it engendered among Germans who were not members of the Party or its auxiliary organizations was a crucial factor in intimidating Hitler's opponents and bringing his sometimes rather unwilling allies into line.[63]

While records are sparse, there were at least hundreds if not thousands of torture centers established by the SA where "enemies of Germany" were tortured and murdered.[64] One of the first concentration camps, the Kemna concentration camp, in an old textile factory in Bavaria, was run by the SA group in Dusseldorf between July 1933 and January 1934. The camp held communists, socialists, trade unionists, and even dissenting Catholics.[65] The torture and treatment of the prisoners was enough to provoke comment from Franz Gürtner, the German Minister of

Justice, who said that the treatment of prisoners by the SA "reveals a brutality and cruelty in the perpetrators which are totally alien to German sentiment and feeling. Such cruelty...cannot be explained or excused by militant bitterness, however great." [66]

THE REICHSTAG FIRE

On February 22, 1933, Hitler was just three weeks into his term as chancellor. He did not yet have dictatorial powers. That day, he ordered 50,000 SA men enrolled as auxiliary police. Two days later they raided Communist headquarters announcing (falsely) that they had found seditious literature calling for an armed revolution and attacks on public buildings.

At 9:00 p.m. on February 27, 1933, passersby heard the sound of breaking glass coming from inside the Reichstag, the home of the German parliament. Flames began to light up the inside of the building. Fire engines ultimately controlled the fire, but not before it had destroyed the debating chamber.

Hitler, Goebbels, and Wilhelm Frick, the interior minister, arrived on the scene and quickly declared that the arson was the result of a communist plot. Hitler turned to Sefton Delmer of the London Daily Express, who had also arrived at the scene of the fire, "You are now witnessing," he said, "the beginning of a great new epoch in German history, Herr Delmer." [67]

The official account of the fire, released by the Nazis and dated February 28, warned of a sinister plot behind the fire:

> The burning of the Reichstag was intended to be the signal for a bloody uprising and civil war. Large-scale pillaging in Berlin was planned for as early as four o'clock in the morning on Tuesday. It has been determined that starting today throughout Germany Acts of terrorism were to begin against prominent individuals, against private property, against the lives and safety of the peaceful population, and general civil war was to be unleashed.
>
> Warrants have been issued for the arrest of two leading Communist Reichstag deputies on grounds of urgent suspicion. The other deputies and functionaries of the Communist Party are being taken into protective custody. Communist newspapers, magazines, leaflets and posters are banned for four months throughout Prussia. For two weeks all newspapers, magazines, leaflets and posters of the Social Democratic Party are banned.[68]

"People behaved as if stunned," a contemporary noted. Apartment houses organized guards against the feared pillaging. Peasants set up watches at springs and wells for fear of their being poisoned. As the propaganda machine fanned the fears of the citizens, the door was opened for Hitler to take advantage of the opportunity.

On February 28, the SA members who had been appointed auxiliary police moved out across the capital, arresting Communist Party activists and taking them to makeshift prisons and torture centers. The lists of those to be arrested had already been prepared. At least 4,000 people were arrested, including many of the 81 Reichstag deputies from the communist party, effectively eliminating the party as a voting bloc in the Reichstag. Within two weeks the number arrested was estimated at more than 10,000. Beside himself with delight at the way things were going, Joseph Goebbels is reported to have commented, "Once again it is a joy to live!"[69]

Also on February 28, on the advice of Hitler, President von Hindenburg signed the Decree for the Protection of People and State Against Communist Acts of Violence Endangering the State, commonly referred to as the Reichstag Fire Decree.[70] The first article removed all fundamental rights explicit in the Weimar constitution, specifically suspending personal liberty, freedom of expression, association, and assembly, and allowing warrantless searches. Habeas Corpus, the requirement that a person under arrest must be brought before a judge or into court, especially when one has been unlawfully detained, was suspended. The second article gave the national government the right to remove state governments. Another article provided the death penalty for violation of the offenses set out in the decree, as well as for committing arson.

On March 23, 1933, with the communist deputies now imprisoned or expelled, the Reichstag passed the Act for the Removal of Distress from People and Reich, otherwise known as the Enabling Act. It allowed Hitler and his cabinet to issue laws without the consent of the Reichstag.

It took one month, and one catastrophic event. The transition from the democratic Weimar Republic to the totalitarian Nazi dictatorship was virtually complete. The stage was now set for Gleichschaltung—the full Nazification of German society.

GLEICHSCHALTUNG: THE INTEGRATION

On 15 April 1933, Joseph Goebbels gave a speech to the press on the newly established Reich Ministry for Popular Enlightenment and Propaganda. Terrorizing roughly half of the population, he said, was not enough:

> If this government is determined never and under no circumstances to give way, then it has no need of the lifeless power of the bayonet, and in the long run will not be content with 52 per cent behind it and with terrorizing the remaining 48 per cent, but will see its most immediate task as being to win over that remaining 48 per cent...
>
> It is not enough for people to be more or less reconciled to our regime, to be persuaded to adopt a neutral attitude towards us; rather we want to work on people until they have capitulated to us, until they grasp ideologically that what is happening in Germany today not only *must* be accepted but also *can* be accepted.[71]

On 23 March 1933, Hitler declared that the primary purpose of Goebbel's new Ministry was to centralize control of all aspects of cultural and intellectual life. "The government," he said, "will embark upon a systematic campaign to restore the nation's moral and material health. The whole educational system, theatre, film, literature, the press, and broadcasting-- all these will be used as a means to this end. They will be harnessed to help preserve the eternal values which are part of the integral nature of our people." [72] It was the Nazi party, of course, that would define those values because, according to Hitler, roughly half of the German citizens who had refused to support the Nazi party had been "seduced" by "Jewish" Bolshevism and Marxism, the "Jewish-dominated" press and media, the "Jewish" art and entertainment of the Weimar culture, and other un-German forces. The people, Goebbels declared, had to start 'to think as one, to react as one, and to place itself in the service of the government with all its heart." [73]

Two weeks later, on 7 April, one week after the beginning of nationwide boycotts of Jewish businesses, the Reich Ministry of the Interior issued the "Law for the Restoration of the Professional Civil Service" (also known as the Civil Service Law), purging all racial and political "enemies" of the regime—Jews, leftists, liberals, and people too independent in their thought—from the German civil service. To "restore a national professional civil service," it said, "civil servants who are not of Aryan descent are to be retired." Similarly, "Civil servants whose previous political activities afford no assurance that they will at all times give their fullest support to the national State, can be dismissed from the service." [74]

The law initially included a clause insisted upon by Hindenburg, exempting those who were veterans on World War

PHASE 3: THE PROPAGANDA OF INTEGRATION

I, or those with a father or son killed in action in the war. This exemption was removed after Hindenburg's death in 1934.

Several days later, a law was passed that defined "non-Aryan" to mean descent from one or more "non-Aryan" grandparents; the law implied that grandparents are to be considered Jewish if they practiced the Jewish religion.

Subsequent orders ended the services contracts of non-salaried Jewish employees of the state, and expelled "non-Aryan" honorary professors and untenured junior professors. Jews who were still protected under the "Hindenburg Exception" could not be advanced in their jobs. Anyone married to a "non-Aryan" could not hold a civil service position.

In the judicial system, judges that were viewed as non-compliant with Nazi laws or principles (i.e. those who delivered unacceptable judgments) were removed. Jewish and socialist judges, lawyers, and other court officers were purged from their professions. The rule of law was dismantled -- judges were instructed to let "healthy folk sentiment" (*gesundes Volksempfinden*), rather than the letter of the law, guide them in their decisions.

Getting the courts in line to the new reality required a process and a restructuring. This was spurred by the findings of the Reichstag Fire Trial. The claim that the Reichstag Fire had been the beginning of a communist plot to destroy the nation was central to the round up, imprisonment, and murder of the communists, and the elimination of the Communist Party in the Reichstag, which in turn had been integral in Hitler being granted dictatorial powers by the Reichstag. In July 1933, four months after the fire, five men were indicted for the fire. One was Marinus van der Lubbe, the unemployed Dutch construction worker who had been found at the scene of the fire. The others included a leading German communist, and three Bulgarian members of Communist International, an international organization founded in 1919 to further communism globally, and led by the Soviet Union. All were in Germany at the time.

On December 23, 1933, to the frustration of the Nazi party leadership, the German Supreme Court found only van der Lubbe guilty, and found the other four not guilty due to insufficient evidence of their involvement in the fire.[75]

Hitler's furious response was to dismantle the Supreme Court, replacing it with the People's Court (*Volksgerichtshof*), manned by judges chosen specifically for their Nazi beliefs, to try treason and other important "political cases." The People's Court would condemn tens of thousands of people as "*Volk Vermin*" and thousands more to death for "*Volk Treason*."

In media, the German radio network was publicly owned, with a 51% stake belonging to the nationwide Reich Radio Company. The other 49% belonged to nine regional stations. Goebbels quickly replaced the two existing Reich Radio commissioners with Nazi loyalists. On June 30, 1933 he obtained a decree from Hitler placing control of all broadcasting in the hands of the Propaganda Ministry. He purged the broadcasting companies, firing 270 people at all levels—13% of all employees—in the first months of 1933. Radio managers and reporters who had been part of earlier liberal broadcasting regimes, including the founder of

PHASE 3: THE PROPAGANDA OF INTEGRATION

German radio, were arrested on corruption charges and taken to concentration camps.

In the early stages, the official communist and social democratic presses were repeatedly banned for offenses real or fabricated. Once the parties were eliminated, the presses were completely closed. On 30 April 1933, the German Newspaper Publishers' Association and the Reich Association of the German Press, the journalists' union, "coordinated themselves" by closing membership to any but the "racially and politically reliable," and appointing executives and council members from the Nazi party. Communist writers, writers deemed radical, and pacifist writers were arrested and taken to makeshift concentration camps established by the SA.

In 1933, 27 art gallery and museum curators were removed and replaced with Nazi loyalists, who had modernist works removed, calling them "Cultural Bolshevism." Others, seeing the prevailing winds, also self-corrected by joining the Nazi party or complying to its policies.

At universities, 1,145 established teachers, 15% of all German professors, were dismissed. In Berlin and Frankfurt the totals were closer to one third. World famous scientists, including 20 Nobel Prize laureates, were dismissed because they were Jewish or had Jewish wives or had been critical of the Nazi regime. These included Albert Einstein, Gustav Hertz, Erwin Schrödinger, and others. Most emigrated and continued their work abroad.

According to Richard Evans, the students themselves drove the "co-ordination process" forward in the universities:

They organized campaigns against unwanted professors in the local newspaper, staged mass disruptions of their lectures and led detachments of stormtroopers in house searches and raids... At Heidelberg University, one Nazi activist disrupted the work of the physicist Walter Bothe by conducting lengthy marching sessions for SS men on the roof of his institute, directly above his office. In one university after another, respected Rectors and senior administrators were elbowed aside to make way for often mediocre figures whose only claim to their new position was that they were Nazis and enjoyed the support of the Nazi students' organization.[76]

And then the book burnings began.

On 10 May 1933, German students organized an 'act against the un-German spirit' in nineteen university towns across the land. They compiled a list of 'un-German' books, seized them from all the libraries they could find, piled them up in public squares and set them alight. In Berlin, at the students' request, the book-burning event was joined by Joseph Goebbels. He told them that they were 'doing the right thing in committing the evil spirit of the past to the flames' in what he called a 'strong, great and symbolic act.' One after another, books were thrown onto the funeral pyre of intellect, to the accompaniment of slogans...

Students had been combing libraries and bookshops in readiness for the occasion since the middle of April. Some booksellers courageously refused to hang up posters advertising the event in their shop windows, but many others gave in to the threats with which the students accompanied their action...

As so often in the history of the Third Reich, the apparently spontaneous action was in fact centrally coordinated, though not by Goebbels, but by the national students' union. The Nazi official in charge of purging Berlin's public libraries helpfully provided a list of the books to be burned, and the central office of the national student union wrote and distributed the slogans to be used in the ceremony. In this way, the Nazi students' organization ensured that the book-burning took a roughly similar course in all the university towns where it was carried out. And where the students led, others followed, in localities across the land.[77]

THE NEW ENEMY WITHIN

By April 1934, a new "outlier" was emerging in the Nazi organization. Ernst Röhm, Chief of the SA, and the person who had overseen and managed its explosive growth, had become too independent in his thinking. He was speaking of "continuing the revolution," replacing the existing elites in the German administration with Nazi party members and merging the German Army into the SA. He had made enemies. Some of those enemies had Hitler's ear.

On June 30, 1934, the leadership of the SA were ordered to Bad Wiesse, Bavaria, for a meeting. As the story has been told, after having cut the telephone communications to and from the hotel so Röhm would not be "tipped off," Hitler himself led the mob of Nazi SS up to the first floor of the hotel where the leaders were staying. Entering Röhm room and catching him having sex with another man, they arrested him. (Hitler reportedly was fully aware of Röhm's homosexuality.) With Röhm gone, the other SA leaders were placed under arrest on manufactured charges of conspiracy to overthrow the government. Over the next three days, in what would come to be known as the Night of the Long Knives, over 150 people, including most of the SA leadership, were murdered. Hundreds more were arrested. Röhm was given the choice of murder or suicide. Refusing to commit suicide, he was shot on July 1, 1934, by two SS guards.

Joseph Goebbels released the news of the arrests and executions to the media, presenting them as a preventative measure to thwart the SA's plans to overthrow the government. On July 13, 1934, the German Reichstag approved a bill retroactively legalizing the purge as emergency defense measures. By 1935, membership in the SA had dropped by 40%.

In the same time period, the Schutzstaffel, or SS, had grown from an elite guard of 3,000 men in 1929, to 209,000 by the end of 1933. On 20 April 1934, the *Geheime Staatspolizei* or *Gestapo*, was put under the SS, setting the stage for the next phase: the Police State.

CHANGING HEARTS AND MINDS

Once the loudest voices of dissent have been silenced, and the others scared into submission, you still will not have achieved uniformity of thought, or uniform alignment to the new ideology. The required "radical change of opinions and behavior as dictated by the new regime," which Mucchielli likens to mass religious conversion, will not be brought about by brutality and fear alone. Controlling education, the media, and the arts is just a start.

The techniques to bring about this "conversion" are more extreme, and Orwellian, than anything we have seen so far. As Nazi Germany did not survive beyond the time span of one generation, it may be more appropriate to look to the Soviet Union or Mao's China as the 20th Century living examples of the more "advanced" methods.

They are all rooted in the ideas emerging from Leipzig in the last half of the 19th century, from Wundt and his successors, that we are little more than animals to be conditioned. As Mucchielli describes:

> The brain, as Pavlov and the researchers of his School showed, is an organ of balance and adaptation between the organism and its environment. By changing the stimuli from the environment, we change the behavioral patterns. Changing the perceptual frame of reference is to force thought to 'reorganize' itself...

It is indeed necessary to start from childhood. The human being must be awakened in the universe prepared for his conditioning, children must learn hymns and prayers before thinking, they must learn to read with the sacred formulas of the great political or religious Messiah, they must learn to write by copying the slogans...and during all this time, it is absolutely necessary that they do not receive contradicting stimuli from their families, or other 'environments', that their group life is controlled, that their memories are constructed with the spatial, social and temporal reference points of the ideological Universe in which one intends to make them live.[78]

THE METHOD

"The one-dimensionality of the environment is an absolute must," Mucchielli says. "Everything must be coherent and carry the same values, the same symbols, the same myths."[79] Achieving this goal requires:

• Control of information and the means of distributing information. Reading materials, mass media, and now, the Internet, must be controlled and government approved. Unofficial sources will need to be suppressed or prohibited until the public receives only official information and official interpretation of events.

• Shaping of the permanent environment. There are points where it is useful to remind yourself that Mucchielli was a psychiatrist, talking to psychiatrists. This is one of those points. Part of achieving integration, he says, is the "reshaping of the perceptive atmosphere" (i.e., the world we see) and completely altering the stimuli coming from the environment. Signs, banners, portraits, slogans, clothing, etc. all provide "suggestion" that makes old habits and reflexes null and void. "Disconcerted, no longer finding his usual reference points, the individual 'deconditions' himself and, being able to adapt only in relation to these new reference points—the only ones that are there—reconditions himself in conformity."[80]

• Restructuring of the human environment. This, Mucchielli says, emerges from research in psychology on the role of groups in creating a person's "personal identity and opinions." Unsettlingly, he says these experimental discoveries have made "new and powerful weapons possible," including:

— Destruction of the previous groups in society, including reducing the role of family cells; controlling or eliminating religious groups and Churches, putting all professional groups under state control.

— Intensification of public life, as provided by the state, including meetings, reunions, parades, festivals, fairs, solidarity days, etc.

— Use, inside groups, of peer pressure to conform, which also helps to identify opponents within the group and single them out for "special treatment."

— Reinforcement of conformist attitudes with rewards, gratification, publicity, and the sanction of nonconformist attitudes.

THE FIGHT AGAINST THE PROPAGANDA OF INTEGRATION.

The problem with fighting the Propaganda of Integration is that the power shift is so far along. If the power of leadership is in the hands of the propagandists, whether in a group, party or nation, repression of dissent can be swift, and radical.

Then Mucchielli delivers the bad news: "The individuals subjected for a sufficiently long period of time no longer have any permeability to counter-propaganda." Then he quotes the words of George Orwell's hero in 1984, "They will not revolt until they have become conscious, but they can only become conscious after they have revolted."

"The great psychological error of a project to defeat this propaganda," he says, "consists in addressing conditioned individuals as if they were discontented, conscious, ready to perceive what seems obvious to those who are not 'in the system.'"[81]

Chapter 8
SOCIAL MEDIA: PROPAGANDA MEETS BIG DATA

If you saw the documentary *The Great Hack* on Netflix, or followed Carol Cadwalladr's articles in the British newspapers *The Observer* or *The Guardian*, you already know that in 2013, a Facebook app called *This is Your Digital Life* paid users $1-2 to take a personality quiz on Facebook. You may even have been one of the 300,000 people who answered its questions. If so, your answers were going to Aleksandr Kogan and Joseph Chancellor, two psychologists and researchers at Cambridge University who had also formed a private company to harvest and sell your data.

If you signed up for the quiz, you probably didn't notice that, when you checked the box, you also authorized Facebook to collect details of all of your Facebook friends. You were told not to worry because they wouldn't collect anything that identifies you personally; they just wanted the demographics. Then they collected every bit of personal data they could get their hands on—user IDs, locations, education, likes, posts, comments, and much more, not only yours but also your friends'. And contrary to their promise of anonymity, they linked every point to users' names and Facebook IDs, and sold the linked data. After adding in the friends, the app developers ended up with personal information on between 50 and 87 million Facebook users.

The name of the Cambridge lab where Kogan, a Moldovan-born US citizen, and Chancellor, an Englishman, did their research was the "Prosociality and Well-Being Lab." According to Kogan—who also publishes under the name Alexsandr Spectre—the focus of their research was to "engineer happiness." Kogan was simultaneously doing private research work with the University of St. Petersburg.[82]

Both men enjoyed a close relationship with Facebook. The social media network had already given them an anonymized, aggregate dataset of "every [Facebook] friendship formed in 2011 in every country in the world at the national aggregate level" for a study on "international friendships." They handed Kogan and Chancellor 57 billion of these Facebook "friend pairs," likely including yours and mine.[83] The results of the experiment, which were published in 2015, were co-authored by researchers at Cambridge, Harvard, and the University of California, Berkeley.

All well and good, aside from the eerie and unsettling idea that Facebook is looking for ways to take charge of my happiness without my knowledge or consent. However, some of the research is more than just interesting. One of Chancellor's research papers found that by exposing a person to awe-inspiring experiences, such as views of the Earth from space, through virtual reality, they simultaneously increased compassion, gratitude, love, and optimism. This would have been less unsettling, perhaps even nice, if they hadn't kept using the word "manipulated" in the paper. But still, the results of this experiment seemed pretty benign.

This all changed in 2013, when three groups of people came together, and Kogan realized the trove of data he was amassing could be used to engineer more than happiness and compassion. And he would make a lot more money in the process. To understand what happened, let's meet the other two groups, the manipulators, and the billionaires.

THE MANIPULATORS

Nigel Oakes, a British businessman who used to own mobile discos, was once primarily known for having dated Lady Helen Taylor, a relative of the British royal family. He made the news in 1985 when he gate-crashed a royal soiree, appalling the Queen,[84] and was escorted out by police.[85] Oakes claims to have studied psychology at University College London, but the university says they have no record of his having been a student.[86]

Oakes had attended Eton, the boarding school of the British elite. Perhaps this explains how in 1987, just two years after the mobile disco king was hauled out of a royal party by the cops, he landed a job at the prestigious international advertising agency, Saatchi and Saatchi, as a senior producer.

Ad agencies have used psychology, and psychologists, to influence the buying habits of audiences since the days of Edward Bernays and Ernest Dichter. (Mucchielli spends the first half of *Psychologie de la publicité et de la propagande* writing about advertising; "Publicité" is the French word for advertising). It was at Saatchi and Saatchi that Oakes became interested in psychology and its potential for manipulating masses of people.

In 1990 he parlayed the knowledge and connections he had gained through his work at Saatchi and Saatchi into a new company of his own, which he named The Behavioural Dynamics Institute (BDI). With funding from a consortium of European investors, Oakes set out to make BDI a leading international center for research and development into persuasion and social influence. He hired two respected psychology professors, Adrian Furnham and Barrie Gunter, to "fill in the blanks of his methodology."[87]

There is very little information available about BDI's operations, its clients, or even the identities of the experts working on its projects. It is known that professors Furnham and Gunter later cut their ties with Oakes, citing several uncomplimentary reasons for doing so. Still, BDI proved to be a stepping stone to Oakes' next venture.

In 1993 Oakes founded Strategic Communications Lab, or SCL, with his brother Alexander, and Alexander Nix, another Eton graduate who has been described as a polo playboy whose father invested in the company. SCL's purpose was to supply "strategic communications, information operations and public diplomacy to governments and military clients around the world." Its approach to propaganda was based upon a "secret methodology" developed by the psychologists at BDI. Steve Tatham, former Commanding Officer of 15 (UK) PSYOP Group, was the head of SCL's defense related business.[88]

Among SCL's first contracts were campaigns in Indonesia and Pakistan (Oakes was forced to leave Indonesia in 2000 after being accused of using "psychological warfare" and illegally funneling money). The company also landed a contract with the Pentagon to conduct surveys in Iran and Yemen. At a global arms fair in London in 2005, SCL billed itself as the first private company to provide psychological warfare services, or "psyops," to the British military.[89] As one person familiar with the company said, "Psysops was big business and people were just chucking money around."[90]

By 2012, SCL was a trusted partner of Britain's Ministry of Defense and was included in the so-called "X List" of companies "cleared for routine access to UK secret information." Among the services SCL provided were military disinformation campaigns, social media "branding," and voter targeting, primarily in the developing world. SCL boasted of its ability to help foment coups.[91] According to documents released by former employee Christopher Wylie, acting Director of Research for SCL and Cambridge Analytica from mid 2013 to late 2014, it was also providing training for Britain's 15th PSYOP Group.[92]

Also in 2012, Oakes formed a subsidiary to SCL, called

SCL Elections, to apply its parent company's "mind-bending" technology to democratic elections. According to a report from the British Parliament in 2017, SCL Elections and its associated companies were involved in elections and referendum campaigns in countries located all over the globe, including Australia, Brazil, the Czech Republic, France, Gambia, Germany, Ghana (2013), Guyana, India, Indonesia, Italy, Kenya (Kenyatta campaigns of 2013 and 2017), Kosovo, Malaysia, Mexico, Mongolia, Niger, Nigeria, Pakistan, Peru, the Philippines, Slovakia, St. Kitts and Nevis, St. Lucia, St. Vincent and the Grenadines, Thailand, Trinidad and Tobago, and the UK.[93]

Oakes appears to have known at least pieces of what Mucchielli writes about. Or he had read enough somewhere to believe he knew. In 1992, describing his work to the trade magazine *Marketing*, he said: "We use the same techniques as Aristotle and Hitler. We appeal to people on an emotional level to get them to agree on a functional level."[94] Wherever Oakes learned the tricks and techniques of manipulating the opinions and behavior of large groups of people, they were deployed by SCL's new subsidiary, Cambridge Analytica.

Cambridge Analytica was created in 2013, specifically to attract political candidates in the US, and to skirt US election laws that forbade foreign groups from working on US elections. Alexander Nix remained a director of SCL Elections while also acting as Cambridge Analytica's Chief Executive Officer. Cambridge Analytica was hired by the Ted Cruz campaign, by John Bolton, and later, by the Donald Trump campaign.

The views that Oakes later expressed on the Donald Trump campaign were revealing. At a Parliamentary hearing in 2018, members of Parliament heard recordings of Oakes speaking to Emma Briant, at the time a senior lecturer in journalism at the University of Essex, where Oakes discussed "the oldest and simplest way of shaping public opinion: stirring up resentment toward a minority group."[95]

Citing an interview with Oakes on November 24, 2017, Briant said that Cambridge Analytica's political campaigns hinged on lies. And, she said, "Oakes recognized this and understood it was not without victims. Indeed, Oakes knew the kind of false messaging they were deploying has had victims before." A transcript of the interview includes the following comment (ellipses are Briant's):

> Sometimes to attack the other group, and know that you're gonna lose them, is going to reinforce or resonate *your* group, which is why, Hitler...I've got to be very careful about saying so...you must never say this...off the record, but...of course, Hitler attacked the Jews because...he didn't have a problem with the Jews at all. But the people didn't like the Jews...so he just leveraged an artificial enemy, well it's exactly what Trump did. He leveraged a Muslim...it *was* a real enemy...ISIS or whatever...but how big a threat is ISIS really to America? I mean, really...we're still talking about 9-11, well 9-11 is a long time ago.[96]

In the same interview, Briant notes that Oakes joked

about Trump manipulating and reinforcing Americans' false belief that Muslim migrants are a threat to their country, a myth propagated extensively by the American Right:

> OAKES: [Trump] also said ridiculous things like, we're going to ban Muslims from coming into the country because I'm sick of people taking machine guns and pointing them at schools…and our children…and our children are the most important thing…Well there's never been a Muslim, ever, that's put a gun on an American school, but it seems to…
> BRIANT: It's the perception.
> OAKES: Yeh, that's terrorism, and they must be Muslims, and there've been a lot of shootings… They're all Americans doing the shootings! And people go 'Yeah, fuck, it's our children! And so you've got Hillary Clinton going 'We're going to increase the fiduciary financial spending and four percent growth in our area…' and people go 'well, you know, good luck with that…I wanna build a wall… [97]

Briant noted that Oakes evokes Hitler's "big lie" theory from *Mein Kampf* in his comments: "Hitler's lie" she said, "presented Germany as 'innocent, besieged' and under attack by the artificial enemy he created—an international Jewish conspiracy, an idea then repeated in Nazi propaganda as they carried out the Holocaust.

Oakes understands the significance of

comparing the messaging [that Cambridge Analytica] put out for Trump to Hitler's disinformation. He told me that Trump secured political control by manipulating an artificial fear of an innocent 'other'—his messaging then propagated by and supposedly 'independent' but coordinated groups. Their methods may seem extreme, but the propaganda themes only resonated because they echoed false beliefs and simplistic explanations for inequality and global insecurity that have been widely disseminated… in US politics and ideological media."[98]

African Americans and Mexicans, according to Oakes, were also easy targets for Trump. Oakes mocked the simplicity of the message compared to the Democrats' dry miscommunications:

"We all thought it was a joke every time he said it. He says that we're going to put up a wall… for the Mexicans… and we were all 'you can't say that!' you know, that's *loony*! 'And then we're gonna get the Mexicans to pay for it,' and the Mexican President's going 'I'm not bloody paying for any of it!' But it didn't matter because in the Rust States the guys were saying 'look, I've got people, the Mexicans coming across illegally, not paying any tax. And he didn't say 'we're going to redress the…' he said 'we're gonna build a wall and keep these fuckers *out*!'"[99]

THE MANIPULATORS MEET THE CAMBRIDGE RESEARCHERS

Alexander Nix became aware of Kogan's research and met Kogan through an employee who attended Kogan's lectures. Nix was particularly interested in the research proving that Facebook profile information could be used to successfully predict a social media user's psychological traits according to a psychometric model called the OCEAN Scale. The OCEAN scale measures an individual's openness to experiences, conscientiousness, extroversion, agreeableness, and neuroticism. It was not new; it was developed in 1988. But marrying it to big data through social media platforms, and adding other available personal information, opened entirely new windows of possibility on knowing who we are and targeting us using our psychological vulnerabilities at a personal level.

Nix wanted to discuss a potential working relationship to commercialize Kogan's research.[100] Kogan already had a software application, CPW Lab (presumably named after Kogan's Cambridge Prosociality and Wellbeing lab), which could be repurposed to harvest profile data from Facebook users. In 2013 Kogan and Chancellor set up a new company, Global Science Research, Ltd. (GSR), to adapt the work of CPW Lab for commercial purposes. The three entities—GSR, Cambridge Analytica, and SCL—came together to marry Nigel Oakes' "psyops" technology with Andrew Kogan's psychometric data, for use on political campaigns in the US.

THE BILLIONAIRE

The work had to be paid for. The financing for the Cambridge Analytica-GSR collaboration came in the form of a $15 million investment from the reclusive computer scientist-turned hedge fund billionaire Robert Mercer. Mercer tends to stay out of the limelight, spending his time sailing in his 200 plus foot high-tech yacht, *Sea Owl*, or tucked into his Long Island estate, *Owl's Nest*. Mercer is an extreme libertarian. Former employee of Mercer's Renaissance Technologies David Magerman said in a Wall Street Journal article that Mercer commented to him that the United States began to go in the wrong direction after the passage of the Civil Rights Act in the 1960s, that African-Americans were doing fine in the 50s and 60s before the act was passed, and that "the only racist people remaining in the US are black." Mercer, according to Magerman, has contempt for the social safety net and wanted to use the money he had made to "shrink government to the size of a pinhead."[101]

By 2013 Mercer and his daughter Rebekah (Bekah) had grown close to Steve Bannon, and had spent or invested tens of millions of dollars in Bannon's strategy to sow distrust of big government and erode the credibility of the major media outlets. They had invested $10 million and received a sizable ownership stake in Breitbart News, a far-right news and opinion website which Bannon once described as a "platform for the alt-right." The site was widely criticized for its inflammatory stories about immigrants, refugees, and radical Islamists. Bannon had assumed control of Breitbart in 2011, with the Mercers' blessing, when its founder

Andrew Breitbart died of a heart attack.

In 2012 Bekah Mercer, who Christopher Ruddy, owner of Newsmax Media once called the "First Lady of the Alt-Right," founded the non-profit Government Accountability Institute, which produced Peter Schweizer's book *Clinton Cash*. The book was made into a documentary by two companies headed up by Bannon, Bannon Film Industries, and the Mercer-backed Glittering Steel.

As the story goes, one day in 2013, a veteran Republican strategist from Wisconsin, Mark Block, started a conversation with the man sitting next to him on a plane. The man turned out to be a cyberwarfare expert for the US Air Force. As Wylie relayed, "the cyberwarfare guy is like, 'Oh, you should meet SCL. They do cyberwarfare for elections.'"[102] He did, and before long, Block found himself sitting with Alexander Nix as Nix pitched Bekah Mercer on Cambridge Analytica's services.

Block described the next steps, and the arrival of Mercer and friends, to *Mother Jones Magazine*:

> Over lunch in Manhattan, Bekah listened intently as Nix gave his pitch. When he finished, she said, 'I really want you to tell this to my dad.' She gave him an address with instructions to meet later that day. At the appointed time, Nix and Block arrived at a grungy sports bar on the Hudson River, north of the city. We're going like, 'What the fuck?' Block says. Bekah texted to say she and her father would soon arrive. Moments later, *Sea Owl*, the Mercer family's 203-foot superyacht, pulled up to

the dock behind the sports bar.

Aboard the yacht, Nix took a seat next to Robert Mercer, opened his Mac, and launched into his spiel again. Bekah sat next to her father on the couch. Behind them stood Steve Bannon...

Whatever Nix told the Mercers that day in 2013, it worked: They agreed to invest a reported $15 million in a new company that would be the face of SCL's American political work. Bannon was given a seat on the board and a stake in the new company, as Nix later said, to help the firm navigate the US political scene. Nix installed himself in Mercer world, presenting himself as Bekah Mercer's political guru and taking meetings at the 'Breitbart Embassy,' the Capitol Hill row house that served as the conservative website's offices and Bannon's crash pad. The company was incorporated in Delaware on December 31, 2013. The name was a mix of old and new: Cambridge Analytica.

Cambridge Analytica quickly signed-on a host of new clients thanks to the Mercers, who leveraged their position as mega-donors to effectively strong-arm politicians into using their new firm. 'It was the Mercers that made people work with us,' an early Cambridge employee told me. Cambridge boasted eight clients at the federal level in 2013 and 2014, and members of the Mercer family have supplied financial backing to each of them, including to five during that election cycle."[103]

The core of Cambridge Analytica's attraction has always been the covertly obtained Facebook identities. Nix claimed to have crunched the Facebook identities and voter registration, credit card histories, their supermarket loyalties, TV watching habits, and much more to create billions of data points. He once told Sky News that "Today in the United States we have somewhere close to four or five thousand data points on every individual." [104]

Like much of what Nix has said, the verification of this claim is a little shaky. But Cambridge Analytica's psychological researchers were indeed able to cluster the data they did have and create psychological profiles that the firm claimed could be applied to break each American citizen into one of five psychological categories, resulting in ads tailored to reach the desired profile. Or as Christopher Wylie put it, "We... built models to exploit what we knew about [people] and target their inner demons. That was the basis the entire company was built on." In his testimony to the US Senate Judiciary Committee on May 16, 2018, Wylie gave more detail:

> Between 2013 and 2015, Cambridge Analytica funded a multi-million-dollar operation called Project Ripon. This project was overseen by Mr. Bannon and was based upon research that was originally conducted by psychologists at the University of Cambridge.
>
> It should be noted that some of the profiling research used as the basis of CA operations had declared funding from the US Defense Advanced

Research Projects Agency (DARPA). The purpose of Ripon was to develop and scale psychological profiling algorithms for use in American political campaigns. To be clear, the work of CA and SCL is not equivalent to traditional marketing, as has been claimed by some. This false equivalence is misleading. CA specialized in disinformation, spreading rumors, kompromat and propaganda. Using machine learning algorithms, CA worked on moving these tactics beyond its operations in Africa or Asia and into American cyberspace.

CA sought to identify mental and emotional vulnerabilities in certain subsets of the American population and worked to exploit those vulnerabilities by targeting information designed to activate some of the worst characteristics in people, such as neuroticism, paranoia and racial biases. This was targeted at narrow segments of the population.[105]

The aim was not always to create votes for the company's candidates. At times it was to suppress voter turnout:

Oftentimes, CA worked to interfere with voter participation, including by weaponizing fear. In one country, CA produced videos intended to suppress turnout by showing voters sadistic images of victims being burned alive, undergoing forced amputations with machetes and having their throats cut in a ditch. These videos also conveyed Islamophobic messages. It was created with a clear intent to intimidate certain communities, catalyze religious hatred, portray Muslims as terrorists and deny certain voters their democratic rights...

I am aware that CA clients requested voter suppression as part of their contracts. CA offered 'voter disengagement' as a service in the United States and there are internal documents that I have seen that make reference to this tactic. My understanding of these projects, which I did not personally participate in, was that the firm would target African American voters and discourage them from participating in elections. Mr. Bannon was Vice President of the company at the time of these voter disengagement projects.[106]

The Cambridge Analytica "pitch," which was seen and heard in *The Great Hack* and elsewhere on YouTube, features Alexander Nix describing the agency's approach. He boasts of a voter disengagement campaign the company ran in Trinidad and Tobago, a Caribbean island nation near Venezuela. The country had two main political parties, one for the Blacks, and one for the Indians. Cambridge Analytica was hired by the Indian party, and went about targeting the Black youth of the island. "The campaign had to be non-political," he said, "because the kids don't care about politics. It had to be reactive, because they're lazy."

They came up with a campaign that was "all about 'Be part of the gang. Do something cool. Be part of a movement." It was called the Do So campaign. What it really meant was "Do So. Don't Vote," as a way to supposedly protest politics, and voting. T-shirts were printed, graffiti appeared on walls, rallies were held, dances were even invented. People started making their own videos, rappers wrote songs. Nix can be heard laughing as he describes the Prime Minister's house being graffitied with "Do So." "It was carnage," he says. "We knew when it came to voting, all the African Caribbean kids wouldn't vote, because they 'Do So.'" The Indian Party, the People's Partnership Coalition, won the election in a landslide.

If there was any question of the character of the team involved in managing our psychological profiles, Wylie describes the work environment:

> When I was at SCL and CA, I was made aware of the firm's 'black ops' capacity, which I understood to include using hackers to break into computer systems to acquire kompromat or other intelligence for its clients. The firm referred to these operations as 'special intelligence services' or 'special IT services'. I have been told about and seen documents relating to several instances where SCL or CA procured hacked material for the benefit of its clients. Some of the targets of these intelligence operations are currently heads of state in various countries. Of concern, some of the former CA staff who worked on these projects currently hold senior positions in the British government. I have also seen internal CA documents that make reference to using specialized technologies and intelligence gathering services from former members

of Israeli and Russian state security services. Mr. Bannon was Vice President at the time of some of these events.[107]

With his professed ability to micro-target and psychologically manipulate US voters, Nix's star rose, as well as his list of US clients. In September 2016, he was a featured speaker at the Concordia Annual Summit in Manhattan—a "highbrow TED-meets-Davos confab"—alongside Madeleine Albright, Warren Buffett, David Petraeus, and New York Senator Kirsten Gillibrand. *Wired* magazine named Nix one of its "25 Geniuses Who Are Creating the Future of Business." In 2017 he spoke alongside Facebook chiefs at the "Online Marketing Rockstars" conference in Hamburg.[108]

The Trump campaign paid Cambridge Analytica over $5 million for its services. Another $1.2 million was paid to the firm by a Mercer-funded super-PAC for an anti-Hillary Clinton campaign. The Facebook campaign launched by Cambridge Analytica forwarded conspiracy theories about Clinton's health and had pictures of handcuffs and prison cells superimposed on her face. Nix has called their work for the campaign "integral" and "pivotal," telling an undercover reporter for London's Channel 4 news that Cambridge Analytica deserved much of the credit for Trump's win. "We did all the research, all the data, all the analytics, all the targeting. We ran all the digital campaign, the television campaign and our data informed all the strategy."[109]

Cambridge Analytica targeted its ads to the profiles they considered "suggestible" in the swing states. Nix would later say that by using Cambridge Analytica's media strategy and Trump's false Islamophobic comments, they were able to deploy fear and resentment where they would be most effective: mobilizing swing state audiences, using voters' personal data to monitor them, and using psychological profiling to manipulate their emotional responses en masse—all in an emerging area of technology that has little to no regulation.

Multiple sources from the campaign have disagreed with Nix's assessment, saying that Cambridge Analytica's role in the Trump campaign was "minimal." We may never know the true extent of the firm's participation in Trump's win because Nix boasts it used a digital form of disappearing ink causing his emails to auto-erase in two weeks. He mocks his clients for not knowing about it.

In 2016, shortly after the Trump election, journalist Carole Cadwalladr was researching fake news. Sitting at her computer one evening, she typed "Are Jews" into Google. It auto suggested "are Jews evil?" She clicked on it and got a page of search results saying they were. "It was a truly jaw-dropping moment," she said. "I then discovered an academic in the US named Jonathan Albright who had just started mapping the fake news network. We had this late-night conversation in which we both quite freaked each other out with what we were finding and he said to me that "companies like Cambridge Analytica can use these fake news sites to track readers around the web."[110] Cambridge Analytica? What's that? The first domino had just fallen.

And then two dissatisfied Cambridge Analytica

employees, Brittany Kaiser and Christopher Wylie, started talking. Their revelations caught Cadwalladr's attention and, along with reporters Matthew Rosenberg and Nicolas Confessore from the *New York Times*, she began digging deeper. They found gold. When the story broke about the inner workings of Cambridge Analytica—including gross violations of US and European privacy laws, and the illegitimate acquisition of the Facebook dataset—the word "explosion" would be an understatement.

Congressional hearings were called in 2018. Among the people subpoenaed was Facebook co-founder and CEO, Mark Zuckerberg, who insisted that Facebook was the victim, that they had been betrayed, and that they would do much better at self-regulating from here on out. Alexsandr Kogan and Christopher Wylie were banned from Facebook. Alexander Nix was forbidden to hold a directorship position in a company for seven years. Carole Cadwalladr collected twelve well-earned awards for her investigative reporting and was a finalist for the 2019 Pulitzer Prize.

But, most importantly, Cambridge Analytica was shut down. Or so we were told. Nigel Oakes continues to bill himself, including on his own LinkedIn page, as a "British behavioral thought leader and defense scientist, whose ideas have laid the foundation for many significant developments both in military influence and population analysis," and a "pioneer in strategic communication."

In February 2020, after the dust had settled, the Trump campaign hired Matt Oczkowski, the former head of product at Cambridge Analytica, in time for Donald Trump's 2020 campaign. Oczkowski now has a company called HuMn Behavior.[111] After the Senate and Parliamentary hearings, the documentary exposé, and the dogged journalists shining a light on the abuses, the link between political campaigns, psychological manipulation, and social media had been cemented, and particularly in the US, was being carried forward unchecked.

WHAT THEY WERE COLLECTING

David Carrol, a New York media professor, was featured in *The Great Hack* as he tried, unsuccessfully, to use the British legal system to find out what data Cambridge Analytica had on him. Just as he was getting close to success, in April 2018, Cambridge Analytica was closed and liquidated.[112]

On September 20, 2020, more than a year and a half after *The Great Hack* was released, London's Channel 4 news paid David a visit.[113] The station had gotten a copy of the Trump campaign's database from the 2016 campaign. And despite earlier assurances and protests from the campaign spokespeople that Cambridge Analytica's impact on the campaign had been "minimal" and they had never used the firm's psychological "OCEAN" model to categorize American voters, there it was, in the entries for Carrol and everyone else (likely including you and me)-- percentages assigned for openness to experiences, conscientiousness, extroversion, agreeableness, and neuroticism—each of the OCEAN characteristics.

But there was so much more. Just as Nix had said, they had crunched the data with other sources to create a massive data trove on every person in the database. In addition to the OCEAN characteristics, Carrol's entry in the database had fields that included whether Carrol had been an early Internet adopter, if he was a heavy Internet user, his magazine subscriptions, his spending habits, including his spending on cars, high tech, the Internet, magazine subscriptions. There were fields with numbers indicating whether he spent money on theme parks, baby products, car products, cruises, diet products, foreign vacations, garden maintenance products, high end electronics, or high end sporting equipment, what credit card rewards programs he had, whether he was a donor to NPR or PBS, whether he was a frequent business traveler, a heavy coupon user, a frequenter of family restaurants, whether he used pay per view, took vitamins, had high value stocks or made high risk investments, and whether he was an impulse buyer. It included whether he liked baseball, basketball, football, soccer, college basketball, golf, tennis, pro wrestling, whether he preferred frozen dinners from home or cooked from scratch, cooked for fun, or was a wine lover, whether he did a lot of online purchases or online travel bookings, whether his credit card usage had been flagged, whether he had written a blog, whether he used voice over the Internet for phone calls, if he used Wi-Fi at home or outside the home, whether he belonged to an auto club or warehouse store, if he was an online gamer or online investor, if he paid bills online or downloaded television shows over the Internet. It tracked whether he frequented specialty organic food stores, had a home office, used business banking, whether he used economy hotels, if he used alternative medicine, and all of the charities he supports.

As he reviewed his file, Carrol commented, "They said 'We didn't do that for the Trump campaign.' Matt Oczkowski, who is currently working for the campaign, said, on the record when asked by a reporter, 'Sorry to disappoint you, but we didn't do psychographics for the Trump campaign.' Well, why do I have one in my file, Matt? It's a level of abuse that we are tolerating in this country. It works as a suppression system."

THAT WAS JUST THE START

In 2023, a consortium of journalists from 30 news outlets, including France's *Le Monde*, Germany's *Der Spiegel*, and Spain's *El País*, accumulated more than six hours of secretly recorded meetings with Tal Hanan, a 50-year-old former Israeli special forces operative who uses the pseudonym "Jorge," and his team members. Hanan's company, Demoman International, is a private service offering to "covertly meddle in elections without a trace," using software that can control 30,000 fake online profiles. According to *The Guardian*:

> Hanan told the undercover reporters that his services, which others describe as 'black ops,' were available to intelligence agencies, political campaigns and private companies that wanted to secretly

manipulate public opinion. He said they had been used across Africa, South and Central America, the US and Europe.

One of Team Jorge's key services is a sophisticated software package, Advanced Impact Media Solutions, or AIMS. It controls a vast army of thousands of fake social media profiles on Twitter, LinkedIn, Facebook, Telegram, Gmail, Instagram and YouTube. Some avatars even have Amazon accounts with credit cards, bitcoin wallets and Airbnb accounts....

Much of their strategy appeared to revolve around disrupting or sabotaging rival campaigns. The team even claimed to have sent a sex toy delivered via Amazon to the home of a politician, with the aim of giving his wife the false impression he was having an affair...

Hanan described his team as 'graduates of government agencies," with expertise in finance, social media and campaigns, as well as 'psychological warfare,' operating from six offices around the world...

In his initial pitch to the potential clients, Hanan claimed: 'We are now involved in one election in Africa...We have a team in Greece and a team in [the] Emirates...You follow the leads. [We have completed] 33 presidential-level campaigns, 27 of which were successful.' Later, he said he was involved in two 'major projects' in the US but claimed not to engage directly in US politics.[114]

While speaking to the undercover journalists, Hanan demonstrated hacking into private Telegram and Gmail accounts with ease. "Today if someone has a Gmail," he said, "it means they have much more than just email," as he clicked through the target's emails, draft folders, contacts and Google drives.

Hanan is far from alone. A 2021 report from Oxford University[115] found that more than 65 firms globally offer online "propaganda as a service." Of those, 48% conducted disinformation campaigns that drive division and polarize citizens. As an example the report cites troll farms in Nigeria with connections to Russia's Internet Research Agency, targeting the US and the UK.

THE ENDGAME

Nazi Germany arose from a strange marriage of experimental and behavioral psychology, the drive for power of Adolf Hitler and the Nazi party, and the drive for money and increased profits from the wealthy businessmen who supported them. The other element was the development of the media tools. Hitler's minister of propaganda, Joseph Goebbels, famously said that Hitler's rise to power could not have happened without radio.

The media tools available to propagandists today would stagger Goebbels. The tools for manipulation through social media, what Mucchielli would call "new weapons," are coming out of psychology departments and psychometric labs of the world's leading universities, and from the social media platforms themselves. New developments in measuring and manipulating us will primarily be used for building a new level of multi-billion-dollar companies and minting new tech billionaires. And as before, unethical men and women will use these tools to find ways not only to shape our buying habits and sell us products we don't need, but to shape our worldviews, opinions, and behavior, as part of reshaping our world to one that is more to their liking, or one that better serves their desires. There will be times when that reshaping could cause us to hate one another, give up our democracies, and even fight each other on their behalf if needed. As in times past, the clients for these technologies will often be wealthy individuals who believe that democracy, and our having rights or a voice in how we are governed, are incompatible with their personal and financial interests, and the politicians they put in place to bring their "new world" into being.

With Cambridge Analytica's trove of 5,000 data points on every American citizen, the field was just getting started. Facebook has filed patents on methods for using the forward-facing cameras on your phone to analyze your expressions and detect whether you're bored or surprised by what you see on their feed. Another method would use your posts and messages, plus credit card transactions and location, to predict if you have a birth, death, or graduation coming up. Yet another uses your phone's microphone to determine which TV show you're watching. Failing that, the social media platform has also filed a patent that allows it to measure the electrical interference pattern created by your television power cable to guess which show is playing, while others predict whether you are in a romantic relationship, your socioeconomic status, and how much you are sleeping.

Does your child use a Meta headset to explore in virtual reality? There are apps that will measure his or her biosignals, that include changes in Electrodermal Activity (EDA), the electrical conductivity of the skin, which changes as emotions change, and changes in his or her heart rate or skin temperature in response to stimuli from the headset, which also of course tracks eye movement to see what is being looked at—all data that will belong to Meta, all of which can be packaged and sold, to advertisers, propagandists, and yes, foreign intelligence operations, to better target you, your opinions, your reactions, and your behavior.

A Facebook spokesman says not to take these patents "too seriously." Take them more than seriously. The potential for the marriage of this level of data with Artificial Intelligence sketches a potentially harrowing future, one not with Cambridge Analytica's 5000 data points per citizens, but millions, with tools for manipulation vastly more effective and ubiquitous than Joseph Goebbels would have ever dreamed. They will add exponential power to the techniques for psychological manipulation that Roger Mucchielli wrote about. They will make Cambridge Analytica look like child's play.

Yes, it could happen all over again, but this time on a scale we have yet to come to grips with. This doesn't mean it has to happen. It does mean that we need to protect ourselves against the growing encroachment.

Chapter 9
WHERE WE ARE

My mother was raised in high society Chicago. When she graduated high school in 1936, like many girls in her community, she went on a grand tour of Europe, with a chaperone. In Munich she watched Hitler speak to a crowd. It was, she said, ominous. His power over the crowd was frightening. She left Germany and continued visiting and shopping around Europe, fell in love with a French actor, and on stern orders from her father and brothers, finally sailed home. Three years later, when Hitler invaded Poland, she was in her junior year at University of Wisconsin.

My father was a student at UCLA studying business at the time. His father had died when he was 12, leaving his mother with five children to raise. They weren't poor. But he had to get clever to cover his college expenses. So he got up early to make sandwiches for other students in his apartment co-op to help cover his room and board. He was a handsome, tanned, avid tennis player. He and his roommates would excitedly peer out the window of their apartment at the two ravishing Hungarian women who lived across the street, Ava and Sza Sza Gabor.

They knew what was happening in Europe, it was well covered in the press. Japan was at war with China and making incursions in Southeast Asia. As with the rest of America, it didn't have any particular impact on them. They carried on with their daily lives. Until, seemingly overnight, the impact on their lives went from zero to 100%.

On December 7, 1941, when the Imperial Japanese Navy attacked the American Naval Base at Pearl Harbor, it was as if the lives they knew ended and different ones began. My father enrolled in a Navy program for upper division college students, the V7 program, which would defer his being drafted until he could finish his studies. Still, he and his fellow students found it difficult to study as the world shifted around them.

It didn't work out as my father had planned. In April, 1943, before finishing his senior year, he was called up, put on a troop train for a training school at Northwestern in Chicago, then shipped out to the South Pacific, where he would be fired on, watch the ship in front of him sink from a torpedo, and see the bodies of young men he had helped to transport floating in the water, lifeless.

My mother saw her four brothers and her father off to active duty, putting themselves in the line of fire in Europe and Asia. Virtually all of her male friends disappeared to war; many never came home. My mother joined the Navy and became a decoder in Seattle.

The generations born after "the greatest generation" were born into a bubble of peace and prosperity unlike any period the world had seen. As the generation of my parents would tell you, that can all change—in the blink of an eye. The one event, or series of events, that could precipitate that change more than any other would be the unraveling of our democracies, which would throw the settling of our differences out of the democratic process and back to the settling of arguments, territories, and power by war. It won't really be in a blink of an eye. We will have had plenty of warning. But if and when it comes, it will feel that way.

When American Congressmen and Congresswomen refuse to commit to accepting the results of an American election, using the same claims of massive voter fraud that were thrown out of 60 court cases after the 2020 election, they are attempting to neutralize the vote, which Mucchielli says is a crucial first step in subverting a democracy, and making it possible for a country to be ruled by a small number of people (see Chapter 5). When Steve Bannon stands before a crowd at Turning Point USA and says that if "they steal this election, and they fully intend to steal it… are you prepared to fight? Are you prepared to give it all? Are you prepared to leave it all on the battlefield?" as he did on June 18, 2024, or when Roger Stone and others openly incite civil conflict to finally eradicate the vote, they are using the exact tactics that Mucchielli spells out to bring it on, including calling up the emotions and symbols of patriotism, the ideals and selflessness of the real defenders of freedom and democracy of our past, when really all they are talking about is killing your neighbors and imploding your own nation to put a politician in office.

When a presidential candidate vows on social media that he will "root out the communists, Marxists, fascists, and radical Left thugs that live like vermin within the confines of our country," and tells his social media audiences that "the threat from outside forces is far less sinister, dangerous, and grave, than the threat from within," as he has repeatedly done, we can't afford to look away from the fact that is using language that could have been taken right out of Roger Mucchielli's book, that it is nearly identical language to that was used to instigate deadly civil conflicts that have collapsed nations and governments in the last century, including Germany, Indonesia, Rwanda, and Myanmar, at the cost of hundreds of thousands of innocent lives; in one case, many millions.

Like my mother shopping in pre-WWII Europe, we may not feel that this threat has a direct impact on our lives. It is only looking at it nearly a century later, with the benefit of history, that we can see that the drumbeat my mother heard at the Nazi rally in Munich was growing, that Hitler's referring to Jews and "leftists" as vermin conspiring to destroy their nation was a part of what would become a dark cloud of hate and bloodshed that would engulf much of Europe in horror. We know now what she didn't know—that it would change everything, and that people she knew would die because of it.

Does this mean you are going to die in civil conflict? No. The United States is not the Weimar Republic, and it is not

Myanmar. But it does mean that we have people attempting to gain leadership of the most powerful democracy in the world who are openly advertising their intent to bring that democracy down, and letting us know they will use force and mass violence if needed. And there are media moguls, tech billionaires, wealthy businessmen, talking heads and members of Congress who are forwarding and supporting them, because they believe they have something to gain from these intentions being realized.

We are my mother in 1939, listening to a charismatic, threatening, denigrating, violent, man, shaken and confused by the hold he appears to have over the crowd.

THE CAVALRY IS NOT COMING OVER THE HILL

I'm afraid this is going to look worse before it looks better. I can only tell you I will not leave this on an entirely bleak note.

Election deniers in Congress, instigators such as Steve Bannon, and foreign governments that are actively working to undermine and weaken our democracy, have only been able to do so today because they are empowered by a base of social media users they can lie to, incite, and agitate, on a daily basis. Keeping in mind that Mucchielli says that the hallmark of propaganda is lies that are easily discredited but continue to be repeated, social media has proven to be an ideal tool to keep followers returning daily to the same troughs for their information—to platforms that have no accountability to truth, where one can launch a lie and watch it being repeated by a continuing stream of "authoritative" voices, even 30,000 bots, until it takes root and becomes something "everyone knows."

This is not limited to supporters of Donald Trump and Steve Bannon. The "spontaneous" growth of antisemitism among crowds on campuses and streets in the US is in some ways more sinister, as the actual instigators are well cloaked, operating on private message chains in encrypted apps, indicating the strong possibility of foreign agents at work against the interests of the US

First in Myanmar and now in the United States, in Europe, India, and elsewhere, social media has delivered a tool that is powerful beyond anything the earlier propagandists would have imagined. And it is, to a degree, our own inaction and our inattention that has put these tools in their hands.

CYBERSECURITY AND THE HACKING OF THOUGHTS AND BEHAVIOR

An entire industry, cybersecurity, has emerged in the last decades to protect your bank account and assets from being hacked by bad actors. Agencies have been formed to protect government assets and infrastructure, as well as companies, and consumers. Magazines and sophisticated websites exist just to report on the field.

There are large, successful companies that train employees to recognize hackers, to spot a phishing email, for instance, and report it and delete it without clicking on the malicious link in the email. They educate users and employees to recognize social engineering (i.e., convincing a user to do something that is against his or her own interests). When you are educated in the tactics, when an email arrives telling you that your daughter's Amazon account is going to be closed if you don't click on this link to verify her account information, instead of clicking on the link and entering your credit card number, address, and social security number, you look at it and say "oh, a phishing email," report it, and delete it. When you are at work and you get an email from the CEO of your company instructing you to change the account number on a payee, you call the CEO's office to verify the account change before implementing it, and likely save the company millions in losses from a scam. This "cybersecurity awareness training" gets remarkable results, creating a culture of security within organizations, and dropping the numbers of people susceptible to clicking on malicious emails or falling for scams down from 59% to, in some cases less than, 4%.

The companies that do this training say that, after malware and malicious email has gotten through all the filters, the end user—the man or woman on the keyboard—is the last line of defense against bad actors.

When it comes to hackers trying to covertly manipulate your political thoughts and behavior, to get you to act against your own interests, you are not the "last line of defense." You are the only line of defense. There is no industry working to protect or even educate us. We are virtually on our own against sophisticated, very well-funded players actively working against us, on both sides of the political fence. Like the hackers who want you to click on their link and unwittingly give them your credit card number or social security number, the job of these "hackers" is to study you and figure out how you can be engineered to do what they want you to do, to vote for who they tell you to vote for, to not vote at all, or to take up arms against your fellow citizens if directed, even when it is clearly against your own best interests.

There is no filter to flag their actions or keep them off your social media feed. There has been no security awareness training. There is no one even thinking about it.

Why are we so undefended?

THE PEOPLE WHO SHOULD BE PROTECTING YOU ARE MAKING MONEY—LOTS OF IT—FROM THE PEOPLE WHO ARE ENGINEERING YOU.

Again for comparison, companies have executives in charge of security, usually a Chief Information Security Officer (CISO). If the company is too small for a CISO, one of the people in tech will oversee security. Part of the job of the security officers is to constantly educate themselves, staying on top of new tech and implementing new and better ways to chase down the hackers and keep them off the company servers. They sometimes get outfoxed. When they do, they come back and find and close the holes and beef the system up so it doesn't happen again.

Imagine that you had a CISO in your company who was taking money from the hackers to let them through, including hackers from other countries who were working to destroy the company. Now imagine that the CISO not only lets them through but actively solicits the hackers;

giving them personal data on the accounts they want to influence, making it easier to manipulate them, because the more the hackers got through, the more money the CISO can put in his pocket.

What would you think if, when the company starts to unravel, the CISO uses the money they have been pocketing to build a bunker on an island to protect themselves from the fallout, while the rest of us suffer the consequences of their actions? You would certainly say that CISO was treasonous to the company.

This is us on social media.

WHAT CAN WE DO?

On an individual level, we can practice our own cyber-security awareness, and use social media wisely. If you have people you don't know among your "friends" and connections on your personal social media feeds, be aware that there is a high chance they are bots or scammers. Unfriend and disconnect. You will lose nothing. Google "how to find out what data *** has on me" on the social media platforms you use, and how to delete your data.

Put no personal information on your profile. Set your privacy settings so no one you don't know can read your feed, so the new phone you bought, your organic dinner, or the fact that you love the new Taylor Swift video doesn't end up in a politician's or a sleazy "election agency's" database.

Fill out nothing on social media that asks you for your name or any form of personal information. Take no surveys, do no quizzes, answer no questions about your personal life. When you click on a link and it takes you to a page that asks for your name, your email, and *any* information, get off the page – fast. Do not sign social media petitions or comment on posts that ask you questions about yourself, your likes, your dislikes, things you remember from your childhood, etc. These are people who are collecting identities for their own purposes and campaigns or fraudulent actions. Engaging with them accomplishes nothing; you lose nothing by skipping over them.

Realize that the social media platforms do not police for fraudulent ads. They make money on them. If you see a celebrity's face selling a product, or a political candidate's picture asking you to donate to an organization you've never heard of, the chances of it being fraudulent are high.

Check your phone's privacy settings to see which apps have access to your full photo library, and limit the access. Your photos have information embedded in them, including location, dates and times. Don't think the social media companies are not scooping this up to use. Tik Tok and Instagram are already using artificial intelligence to gather data about you and your relationships from the photos on your phone.[116] You gain nothing from this and lose nothing from cutting off access and protecting your privacy.

Social media is dead as a source of news. The cacophony of intrusion and manipulation, the false stories posted by false journalists showing false videos is already deafening and is growing louder. Find news sources you trust and get your information from them. *The Guardian* in London covers a lot of territory the US media ignores. I have written for *The Hill* and can tell you that they are dogged about fact checking and insist on credible documentation of anything I have represented as fact. Associated Press and Reuters, because they are read internationally, tend to have less political slant. *Politico* has broken important stories; when they have slipped they have been open about it and corrected it, which is valuable.

Skip the comments. The bots and impostors are busiest on the comments on posts, where they can "piggyback" on topics to inject their message. As an example, I recently read a story about an airplane that was taking off and had a tire blowout. This is a story of high interest to anyone who flies. In the comments, the office of a congressman posted a picture of an airplane against an ominous, threatening sky, and a headline saying that the Democrats are allowing terrorists to pour into our country through the airports. They had "piggybacked" onto the airport story by tying their posts to keywords like "airport" and "danger," thinking that because of the story I was reading, I would be likely to be frightened by their post. In reality, security and border control procedures at airports has been essentially unchanged for the last 22 years, through four presidential administrations. If anything, advanced computerization and facial recognition has made the airports more secure. The post had one purpose – to make you feel afraid. It had used my interest in a subject to manipulate me.

Comments from people you don't know generally have little value. You lose nothing by skipping over them.

Most important, learn the language of hate and agitation as it is laid out in this book. Learn to recognize it and reject it, just as you have learned to recognize and reject a text message that says you won the Publisher's Clearinghouse Sweepstakes, or a package can't be delivered to you until you verify some personal information.

TAKING YOURSELF BACK FROM THE BOTS

Mucchielli devotes the first half of *Psychologie de la publicité et de la propagande* to advertising, and the use of the same psychological techniques that are used in propaganda, but to manipulate what we want to get us to purchase the products of the corporation. In his discussions of the psychological mechanisms used by both advertisers and propagandists, he uses the terms "extro-determined" and "intro-determined." Both advertisers and propagandists, he says, have the goal to move us from "intro-determined," or guided by our own ideas, our own desires, our own values and goals, to "extro-determined," which is wanting the products or leaders they want us to want, having the ideas, and behaving as we are told by the media they feed to us. If Mucchielli could only see us today, unable to make it through a dinner with friends without scrolling on our phones, I believe he would be amazed at their success.

We are not going to throw away our phones, and we are not going to suddenly shut off our social media platforms. We can adjust our usage so that, as above, we are interacting with friends and people we care about, enjoying music or comedy from people who make us feel good or make us smile or laugh instead of those trying to manipulate us. At the same time, we can do, and nurture, those things that are "ours," that are "intro-determined."

Do something every day that comes from you. If you have a job you enjoy, or family members you care for and enjoy communicating and sharing with, you are already well down that road. (These are also the things that Mucchielli calls "bulwarks" against propaganda). There are other ways to use what's inside of you instead of what is fed to you. Learn a language. Build a garden and work in it regularly. Read great fiction stories. Travel places you have always been curious about. Go for a walk every day without your phone. Follow the advice of Kurt Vonnegut when he was asked by a schoolteacher, Mrs. Lockwood, to give advice to her students:

> Practice any art, music, singing, dancing, acting, drawing, painting, sculpting, poetry, fiction, essays, reportage, no matter how well or badly, not to get money and fame, but to experience becoming, to find out what's inside you, to make your soul grow.
>
> Seriously! I mean starting right now, do art and do it for the rest of your lives. Draw a funny or nice picture of Ms. Lockwood and give it to her. Dance home after school, and sing in the shower and on and on. Make a face in your mashed potatoes. Pretend you're Count Dracula.
>
> Here's an assignment for tonight, and I hope Ms. Lockwood will flunk you if you don't do it: Write a six line poem, about anything, but rhymed. No fair tennis without a net. Make it as good as you possibly can. But don't tell anybody what you're doing. Don't show it or recite it to anybody, not even your girlfriend

or parents or whatever, or Ms. Lockwood. OK?

Tear it up into teeny-weeny pieces, and discard them into widely separated trash receptacles. You will find that you have already been gloriously rewarded for your poem. You have experienced becoming, learned a lot more about what's inside you, and you have made your soul grow.[117]

If it really came down to it, you could live without social media. You don't have to. But spending more time with family and friends without your phone, or time spent doing something creative or something you enjoy just because you enjoy it, will put more of your "self" in your own hands and less of you in the hands of unscrupulous social media operators.

IN THE GLOBAL PICTURE

On the larger scale, there are two points Mucchielli makes that will form the shape of the road ahead of us:

A: Mucchielli stresses that the power in these psychological techniques lies in their being undetected. Making them known deflates their power. He repeats this twice in his book.

We need writers to write about what Roger Mucchielli wrote about, about the men in Leipzig who laid the foundation for it, the manipulators who have used it to get citizens to hate and kill. We need film makers to make films about it, speakers to speak about it.

We need industrious magazine publishers to start magazines for the field similar to the commercial cyber security magazines, but calling out propaganda efforts around the world, how they are doing it, and the impact. We need enough people to read and watch to keep these publishers and reporters alive so they can keep the public informed on an ongoing basis.

We need curriculum writers and app developers and bright technical minds to pass on and be creative with the understanding Mucchielli has made available to us. Social media founders and executives, their investors, and the psychologists they hire, have become millionaires and billionaires by using us, our lives, our personal data, our thoughts, our habits, and our behavior, as a commodity, with no conscience or morality regarding the effects or ramifications on our lives. We need to be smarter and more creative from the other side, to re-empower social media users, to educate and raise our awareness and our ability to spot and upend manipulation. Mucchielli gave us the framework and the signposts. It is up to us how we use them.

B: The other point that Mucchielli makes is that after people have been exposed to this form of propaganda for too long, they become essentially "impermeable." These are people who have been so immersed in the propaganda that they believe that anyone who doesn't share their beliefs is on the "other side," the "enemy." Unfortunately, a number of these people are stocking up on ammunition and training at firing ranges on weekends for the coming "showdown." Worse, they include the veterans and their trainees who are doing military drills in urban warfare in rural areas of the United States at this moment, "standing back and standing by" for orders to go into action. There are politicians who are waiting to forward that signal to action, who believe they have too much to gain from the new regime to stop and look at the future they are helping to create.

Realistically, point B could get ugly, regardless of election results. There are leaders and advocates promising that it will get ugly. We should believe that they are serious. This doesn't mean believing that they will show up at your door with a machete or AK-47. It also doesn't mean believing that every person who votes Republican is in favor of violence in the streets—by far. It means believing, when Kevin Roberts, President of the Heritage Foundation, says that American right "is in the midst of a second American revolution, and it will be bloodless if the Left lets it be," that this person intends to create violent chaos to get the power he desires. And he has been having enough conversations with others on the subject that he feels confident making such a proclamation in public.

Continuing A will still be the ultimate solution. But with B in mind, I will pass on the words of a Jewish art dealer I did a writing project for once. "One thing the Jews have learned over the years," he said, "is always keep your passport in order, and always have some cash where you can easily get your hands on it."

THE HOPE

I had a chapter in this book on the Soviet Union, specifically on how they implemented Phase 3, the Propaganda of Integration. I tossed it out just because it was so dark—all about conditioning masses and creating a new breed of man and woman out of the hollow shells who had had their previous selves conditioned out of them. I could barely read it myself. I will include it in summary here, because I do like the ending. Bear with me as I try to condense more than 70 years of history into a few pages. For those who would like a deeper look into the Soviet years, I strongly recommend Timothy Snyder and Anne Appelbaum, both of whom have written extensively and beautifully about the region and its history.

As you will recall, the essence of Mucchielli's Phase 3, which happens after the overthrow, is to create uniformity of thought. This cannot happen without silencing the opposition. Mucchielli says there can be no exceptions. Fail in this step, and your opposition will not only continue to open their mouths; they will write things that become popular and build followings; they will organize actions against you. In all of the cases of Mucchielli's propaganda in action in the last century, silencing these voices has been done by mass executions and some form of concentration camp or prison camp.

Two waves of "Red Terror" were launched by Soviet leaders against the "enemy within." After the revolution in 1917, there was opposition to the new regime, not only from the White Army, which openly fought the Red Army, but also from factions that had played a part in the toppling of the Tsar but had their own ideas.

On August 30, 1918, Vladimir Lenin was shot after attending a speaking event. As he was recovering in the hospital, he wrote to one of his operatives, telling him that "It is necessary secretly–and urgently–to prepare the terror." It was a signal to begin a campaign of brutal suppression against the Bolsheviks' "class enemies." Between 1918 and 1921, the campaign of terror would end with more than 100,000 people who had been deemed "counterrevolutionaries" --monarchists, social democrats, clergy, foreigners and others -- being executed in mass shootings and hangings, most without trial, in Soviet Russia, Soviet Ukraine, and in Bolshevik-occupied Latvia, Lithuania, Estonia, and Finland.

Between 1932 and 1933, when the Ukrainian farmers objected to losing their farms and being forced into government run "collectives," the Soviet response was the Holodomor (Ukrainian for "death by hunger"), the forced starvation of 15 million Ukrainian farmers, their families, and their villages. Soviet soldiers entered the farms and confiscated not only the crops, but the seed for the next crop; in the homes, they literally took the food from the cupboards. People killed their own children rather than watch them starve before their eyes. The dead were thrown in mass graves, with no one left to mourn them.

A second wave of mass executions began in 1936 and continued through 1938. Joseph Stalin had nearly a million Soviet citizens executed in what he called the Great Purge. Leading members of the Communist Party, including some of its founders, were arrested as counterrevolutionaries; they signed forced confessions and were executed as traitors. Hundreds of thousands were arrested and executed or sent to the gulags (forced labor camps), where they perished. Victims of the purge included more than a third of the Communist Party's rank-and-file members, and over half of the Central Committee. Nearly all of the highest-ranking military leaders (81 out of 103) were tried and executed.

Also caught in the net were massive numbers of ordinary citizens. During the Purge, people denounced their friends, coworkers, and even family members. Academics, artists, musicians, writers, and scientists were arrested and killed, including those who had supported the Bolshevik Revolution. The actual number of those killed is not known, but scholars believe it was well over 750,000. In the end, the head of the NKVD, the Soviet secret police force that had carried out the arrests, forced confessions, and executions, was himself arrested and executed.

As the battle against the "enemy within" is underway and the opposing voices are being effectively silenced by death, imprisonment, or fear, the uniformity part of Phase 3 is accomplished by complete control of the "stimuli" around the individual, not only through the media, but, in the case of Russia, government control of the statues, murals, and billboards, the decorations within the homes. Recalling that Mucchielli says that by altering the stimuli around a person, you alter the brain, and "force thought to reorganize itself" could lead one to wonder if the Soviet Union and Mao's China were enormous psychological experiments, rooted in the views of Wundt, Watson, and Skinner that we humans are little more than brains and neurons responding to stimuli, and believing that by complete conditioning, they could shape the thought of their citizens according to their dictates. Certainly for the Soviets, "conditioning" was a tool and a vital element in the engineering of the "new Soviet man."

In the 1950s, Joseph Stalin explored additional means of mass conditioning, elevating Pavlov in the Russian sciences in the process. In 1954 when he died, having deemed that words are "triggers" for responses, he had a project underway to rewrite the Russian dictionary.

Fast forward to the mid-1980s. The Soviet economy was sinking under the weight of its bureaucratic apparatus, economic stagnation, and the death of three elderly leaders in just two years. On March 11, 1985, Michael Gorbachev, the former Secretary of Agriculture, was elected General Secretary of the Communist Party of the Soviet Union by the Politburo, the Soviet Union's supreme policy making body. A member of the Central Committee of the Communist Party since 1971, Gorbachev had come up through the ranks. He was the youngest member of the Politburo.

In 1985 Gorbachev introduced Perestroika, a restructuring of the Soviet economy intended to breathe vitality into the country by attracting foreign corporations and taking halfway measures toward a market economy. The result was financial chaos, which produced the growth of the primary threat to integration propaganda: discontent.

Instead of eliminating the voices of discontent as his predecessors had done, in 1986 Gorbachev introduced Glasnost, a policy of openness to be applied to political and social issues. His actions were the opposite of Mucchielli's integration propaganda. Glasnost loosened state control on media and the arts, and opened the door for open criticism of the government in Soviet media. Literature that had been previously censored was made available again. Former dissidents and prisoners —including Nobel laureate physicist and activist Andrei Sakharov—were allowed to return from exile and even run for office in the Congress of People's Deputies.

In the Soviet bloc countries, as the voices of discontent rose unsuppressed, demonstrations by groups opposed to Soviet rule began, first in Poland under the leadership of Lech Walesa and the Solidarity movement, quickly followed by Hungary, Czechoslovakia, and East Germany. When Gorbachev pledged that the Soviet Union would not respond militarily to preserve the Communist regimes in the Eastern bloc, long-suppressed hopes for freedom began rising across the region.

On August 23, 1989, more than two million citizens formed a human chain, the "Baltic Way," through Estonia, Lithuania, and Latvia, demonstrating for government transparency and a restoration of independence.

On November 4, 1989, more than half a million people gathered at East Germany's Berlin Wall, the wall that had locked them under Soviet Rule since 1961, and one of the most potent symbols of Soviet Rule to the West. In an attempt to calm the protests, East German leaders announced the they would ease travel restrictions to the West. Government spokesperson Günter Schabowski announced the new rules to stunned journalists at a press conference. Pressed for details, Schabowski , who had not had time to fully read his brief, erroneously said that as far as he knew, the restrictions were lifted effective immediately.

The news hit the media and East Germans flocked to the wall. Realizing that a few border guards were ineffectual against such a crowd, and with no clear instructions from his superiors, Harald Jäger, a border guard, gave the order to open the barrier.

The world was glued to television sets as East Germans flowed through the border, some crying, some celebrating, as they were greeted by West Germans. Some arrived with pick axes and hammers and began picking away at the wall. For those of us who had lived in fear of the Soviet Union for most of our lives, the world had turned a page.

Three months later, on February 7, 1990, the Soviet Communist Party accepted Gorbachev's recommendation and voted to end one-party rule, ending its monopoly on power and opening the government to direct political opposition. On June 12, 1990, elections were held and Boris Yeltsin became Russia's first popularly elected president. The same day Yeltsin signed a Declaration of State Sovereignty by the Russian Soviet Federative Socialist Republic, which stated that the Russian constitution would now take priority over Soviet legislation, that citizens would have equal legal opportunity, and establishing the separation of legislative, executive, and judicial powers.

Seven months after the Baltic Way protest, on March 11, 1990, Lithuania became the first Soviet republic to declare independence. In the following months Latvia and Estonia followed suit, rapidly joined by Armenia, Moldova,

Ukraine and Georgia.

Just two years after the fall of the Berlin Wall, in August, 1991, hardliners from the Communist Party of the Soviet Union, angry at the reforms and loss of the Eastern European states, dispatched KGB agents to Gorbachev's dacha, detaining him, his wife and daughter. But the page had already been turned. More than 250,000 Soviet citizens gathered in protest outside the White House, the Russian Parliament building, and other government buildings, demanding an end to the coup and the establishment of a democratic Russia.[118] When tanks were sent in to disperse the protesters, many of the tank drivers switched sides to join the protests; instead of shooting protesters, they used their tanks to protect the demonstrators. An additional 200,000 protesters surged into the streets of Leningrad, and 400,000 more in Kishinev, the capital of the Moldovan Republic.[119] The coup failed and Gorbachev was returned to Moscow.

Four months later, on December 26, 1991, Mikhail Gorbachev resigned as President of the Union of Soviet Socialist Republics, and formally disbanded the USSR. The hammer and sickle flag of the USSR was lowered for the last time outside the Kremlin building and was replaced with the flag of Russia.

The collapse of the Soviet Union begs a question. We have seen the Propaganda of Indoctrination and Recruitment, and the Propaganda of Agitation, work, and produce the desired result. So the Propaganda of Integration, as Mucchielli outlines it, should have delivered—through the suppression of opposition, the scapegoating, control of stimuli, and other elements of mass conditioning—uniformity of thought in a population. Yet it took only six years from the beginning of the loosening of controls (i.e., easing the actions of the Propaganda of Integration) for the streets to fill with protesters who would topple the entire empire while demanding their freedom.

Where did these three million protesters come from? They were adults, who had lived their lives under the strictly controlled Soviet environment. They had grown up in Soviet schools building shrines to Lenin. As they aged, they were forbidden to travel. Their exposure to opposing viewpoints was virtually blocked, while their lives were saturated by Soviet propaganda—parades, posters, schoolbooks, art, news, radio, and television. The conditioning of Soviet citizens had by this time been going on consistently for three or four generations. Why were the citizens not behaving according to the conditioning they had been raised with?

Perhaps the citizens of the USSR hadn't been conditioned at all. Perhaps their desire for freedom was simply suppressed by fear—the terror of a KGB truck pulling up in front of their house in the middle of the night, the terror of the gulag; the terror of the firing squad—supported by a confusing flood of propaganda lies. In the end, it could not be killed. When they would no longer be sent to the gulag for having an original thought, or have tanks crush their demonstration for freedom, maybe most importantly, when they had access to information from outside the Soviet Union, these protesters could not throw off their shackles fast enough. Perhaps what we witnessed, in this one slice of history, was the abject failure of the theories and attempts in "mass conditioning" that had been at the heart of the Soviet experiment.

At the very least these events would suggest that the desire for freedom and dignity cannot be so easily, and so methodically, conditioned out of us, that perhaps John B. Watson was dead wrong in saying that there "is no difference between man and brute," that perhaps there is more, perhaps even much more, to us than they knew or would admit.

One of my favorite stories of the Gorbachev era is that of four young men laying on the floor of a cathedral and listening to the Beatles for the first time, and weeping. Perhaps it will be art that takes us there and relights the spirit that will take us through the dark period and into a brighter day.

APPENDIX

I cannot say why the psychological techniques of collapsing and overthrowing a nation are not being taught in history, political science, and mass communications classes. I don't know why when you search for "Propaganda" on Amazon, you get 306 books, and none of them have this information in them. Some, such as Bernays' book *Propaganda,* have pieces of the picture. None tell the story that Roger Mucchielli knew. I am not sure why a book as relevant to our last century as *Psychologie de la publicité et de la propagande* was tucked away in a technical and scientific library in Paris, France, categorized as "Advanced Studies in Psychiatry," or why it was never translated into English.

I do know that throughout our last century, there

have been people who knew what Mucchielli knew. We know this by their work, and their results. The stories of how they were used are not easy to read, and much more difficult to fully grasp. This is why, other than brief mentions in the text of the book, they are in an Appendix instead of the body.

Hitler and Goebbels used the developments in the new fields of experimental and behavioral psychology to create a wave of horror that engulfed Europe. It wasn't just propaganda, though that played an enormous part in Hitler's rise and creating the cheering, flag waving Jew-hating crowds. Gustave Le Bon (who, I remind you, Hitler drew from in *Mein Kampf*) and other psychologists from the era introduced the "scientific finding" that our characteristics, including intelligence, character, and ability – and so our value – are solely genetically determined, or determined by physical characteristics from the color of one's skin, to the laughable "size of one's head. This means entire races are inherently and unchangeably inferior, which opens the door to the "engineering" of the new German race by elimination of the "inferiors," initially by eugenics and ultimately by gas chambers.

Eugenics and the Holocaust are not part of the subject matter of this book. But the same developments in psychology that have enabled mass psychological manipulation by propaganda played no small part in what the Nazi leadership became, and the events we are already so familiar with that followed.

The far-reaching effects of this fundamental shift in

the definition of who we are as human beings have not been fully chronicled. As one example, Hendrik F. Verwoerd, a South African politician and psychologist, studied in Hamburg, Berlin, and Leipzig, in the 1930s. On his return to South Africa, he became Prime Minister, and the architect of South Africa's cruel apartheid system.

Fewer people are familiar with what happened in Indonesia in 1965 and 66, in Rwanda in 1994, and in Myanmar (formerly known as Burma) between 2012 and 2018. I have not gone into these at any length in the book. Each could be the subject of an entire book; and there are excellent books on each subject. But it is difficult to understand the impact of the ways these propaganda techniques were used in these nations, and the horrors that resulted, without knowing at least a cursory history.

INDONESIA

In 1965, mobs of Indonesian citizens, spurred on by frantic fear that the "enemy within," in this case the legally registered and sanctioned communist party, was going to destroy their nation, their religion, and all that they held valuable, began killing members of the country's Left, using whatever was at hand—knives, sickles, machetes, iron rods. They were, they believed, being patriots, and saving the nation by eliminating the "cancer" that was strangling the country. The killing accelerated and expanded until more than 600,000 were dead (by some reports it was over 1 million). The killing was so massive there were stories of corpses clogging the rivers and stream. Another million were incarcerated.

We were in the thick of the Cold War. Lyndon B. Johnson had been sworn in as President the year before; he had raised the number of troops in Vietnam from 75,000 to 125,000, ostensibly to hold back the danger of China sweeping through Southeast Asia and into India. The Western powers needed strong allies in the region to act as bulwarks to communist expansion, which could potentially sweep into Southeast Asia and down into India. They envisioned a military alliance of Asian nations similar to NATO to hold back China's expansion.

Sukarno, the founder and President of Indonesia, the fourth most populous nation in the world, was walking a delicate line diplomatically. While he maintained relationships with Western leaders, Sukarno was also friendly with the leaders of Communist China and the Soviet Union. After a visit to China in 1956, he had publicly admired the economic progress made by the nation under communism and praised the effectiveness of the highly centralized government.[120] He also routinely visited the White House and addressed the US Congress, and traveled to Moscow for state visits with Premier Khruschev.

In 1961 Sukarno was a founding member of the Non Aligned Movement, a coalition of nations, also including Yugoslavia, Egypt, India, and Ghana, that called on its members for "abstention from the use of arrangements of collective defense to serve the particular interests of any of the big powers." By the 1960s, Sukarno had allowed the country's communist party, the *Partai Komunis Indonesia* (PKI), to grow as a legally registered and government sanctioned political party. Now it was the third largest communist party in the world, second only to China and the USSR.

In September 1963, the British Crown colonies of North Borneo, Sarawak, and Singapore joined with the independent Federation of Malaya to become Malaysia. (Singapore was expelled from the union two years later). Sukarno opposed the union, saying it was British imperialist expansion in the region, and a low-level armed conflict ensued. Malaysia was militarily backed by the United Kingdom, Australia, and New Zealand. Indonesia received indirect support from China and the USSR. To Western eyes, as players on the chess board of the Cold War, Indonesia was precarious. It was decided that Sukarno had to go.

Documents declassified in 2021 show how the British Foreign Office's cold war propaganda arm, the Information Research Department (IRD), led a team to agitate for the overthrow of Sukarno, using the same tactics that you have been reading about here, to incite the hatred and the fear of the country's destruction, to set the killing in motion, and to inflame it once started.[121] British operatives disguised themselves as Indonesian expatriates and planted false news stories with nationwide radio stations. They swept the nation with the call to destroy the PKI, demanding that "in the name of all patriotic people that this communist cancer be cut out of the body of the state." They sent hundreds of inflammatory pamphlets inciting citizens to kill the left wing foreign minister Dr. Subandrio.[122] To the large Muslim population they sent pamphlets saying that the communist agents of China would take over and destroy

Indonesia and the Muslim religion. The citizens were unaware that these were the work of the United Kingdom.

Just as the Reichstag Fire had propelled Hitler from Chancellor to dictator, the "catastrophic event" that pulled the trigger and released the now agitated mobs into violence was the so-called 30 September Movement's attempted coup. As the story goes, believing that seven of the army's generals were going to attempt a coup against Sukarno, in the early hours of October 1, 1965, members of the Indonesian National Armed Forces (the Air Force and Army) in Jakarta kidnapped and killed six of the generals (the seventh escaped), declaring that they had taken control of the army.

Their moment was short lived. General Suharto, a right-wing US and British ally, was commander of the army's strategic reserve. He quickly assumed control of the military; by the early morning hours of October 2, the coup was over. Suharto then began the first steps in wresting control of the government from Sukarno.

Suharto declared that the attempted coup was the work of the communist PKI. A new propaganda campaign was released saying that it had been the tip of a nationwide conspiracy by the PKI to commit mass murder. Doctored graphic images and descriptions of the generals being tortured, murdered, and castrated went out across the country. Others were sent out with the story that female PKI agents had lured the generals with sexual dances only to gouge their eyes out. On October 5, the story went out in the army paper *Angkatan Bersendjata* that the generals had been subjected to "barbarous deeds in the form of tortures executed beyond the bounds of human feeling." The story was picked up by other national papers and became an integral part of the new campaign. They didn't mention that on October 3, the bodies of the generals had been exhumed from the well they had been thrown into and immediate autopsies had been done. The kidnapped generals had been shot at point blank, with no evidence of torture or mutilation.

The communications equipment required to get the message out nationwide was supplied by the CIA.[123] In a telegram back home on October 5, the US ambassador urged clandestine propaganda efforts to "spread the story of the PKI's guilt, treachery and brutality" as the "most needed immediate assistance we can give [the] army."[124]

The PKI leaders were quickly rounded up and arrested. Most were executed. Public demonstrations were organized by the Indonesian military; at one demonstration the PKI's headquarters was burned. Youth were organized into militia, including the Students' Action Front (KAMI), the Indonesian Youth and Students' Action Front (KAPPI), and the Indonesian University Alumni Action Front (KASI). Anyone aligned or even sympathetic to the PKI was painted as an enemy intent on destroying the nation—even illiterate peasants in remote villages were accused of participating in the plot.

The killings began in October 1965, in Jakarta, and spread to Central and Eastern Java, Bali, and other parts of Indonesia. The targets of this violence grew to include not only PKI members, but anyone "left leaning," including writers, artists and university professors as well as ethnic

Chinese, trade unionists, atheists, and others. In some cases, the killing was used to settle old unrelated scores.

As Vincent Bevins described in *The Atlantic* in 2017:

> In Central Java at the *Sekretariat Bersama* 1965, one of Indonesia's main organizations for the remembrance of these events, I met a survivor of the 1965 massacre. 'I believed in President Sukarno and our revolution. At the time our country had the official 'NASAKOM' ideology, which meant that Nationalists, Muslim groups, and Communists were all supposed to work together to build the country,' he said. 'Yes, I worked on the left side of politics, broadly under 'KOM,' and there was nothing wrong with that.'
>
> Though he worked as a schoolteacher and not as an actual PKI member, he said he was arrested and tortured for days, before watching his cellmates dragged off one by one, never to return. He was spared, for reasons he never understood, and spent over a decade in prison. But it wasn't only communists and leftists who were victimized. Untold numbers of people were tortured, raped, and killed because someone simply accused them of being communists, or for belonging to an ethnic minority, or simply being an enemy of some member of the officially-sanctioned death squads.[125]

As the massacres progressed, the British propaganda

unit continued to feed and accelerate the killing. "We are fighting for our lives and the very existence of Indonesia," one such message read, "and we must never forget that. THE CATS ARE WAITING TO POUNCE."

By the time it was over, bodies were literally clogging rivers into some Indonesian cities. Democracy in Indonesia, or as some have called it, Sukarno's pseudo-democracy, hard-won after two centuries of colonization, was also dead. Suharto would lead the new regime as a military dictator, with the blessing of the West, for the next 30 years.

In the declassified documents, the UK's IRD boasted that, using limited tactical "psywar measures" and black propaganda, they had pulled off "one of the most successful propaganda operations in postwar British history."

RWANDA

If you were alive in 1994, and caught the covers of the news magazines, read the *New York Times* or listened to the BBC, you may know Rwanda as the West African nation where in 100 days, between April 7 and July 15, ethnic Hutus in Rwanda murdered somewhere around 800,000 of their countrymen, the ethnic Tutsi group—mostly hacking them to death with machetes or clubbing them to death. (Some say it was 500,000 killed, others say more than a million. When you are in the hundreds of thousands of dead, the exact number probably doesn't matter). You may remember the photos of lines of corpses draped in canvas, or the piles of skulls in the memorials.

Like many, if you know about Rwanda at all, you

probably believe that the killing was an explosion of African tribal rivalries, perhaps exacerbated by the Belgian colonizers. This was not the case. As one expert on the genocide said, it was "a genocide fully as modern as the Holocaust in the sense that it was state organized, and state driven."[126]

Rwanda has a history of tensions and even massacres before 1994, but they were nowhere near the scale of 1994. Before the genocide, in the cities and villages, life in Rwanda was not about power struggles or even ethnic differences. If you were a Hutu woman who married a Tutsi, you became a Tutsi, and vice versa. So you could be a Tutsi woman with a Hutu sister. Your children may be Tutsi, your nieces and nephews Hutu. Your kids went to the same schools, you sang in the same choir in Church, you shared meals. The two groups were so intermarried that even the physical ethnic distinctions were fading.

Then one day, if you were a Tutsi, your neighbor started to look at you suspiciously. You no longer shared meals. Maybe your kids got beat up at school and called names. One day you may have heard the term *inyenzi* (cockroach) muttered under someone's breath (the ever-present comparison of human beings to insects or vermin). You heard things on the radio that the time for the Tutsi to be "finished" was coming. It was frightening. But by the time it came, and your neighbor or someone two blocks over from your house became possessed to kill you, it was too late to leave. There was no way out.

The Rwandan genocide was not a natural outgrowth of anything. It was engineered, over four years, by a group of

"Hutu Power" extremists in the government and powerful Rwandan businessmen who flooded the news and the airwaves with propaganda. Phase 1 of the campaign started with the newspaper, *Kangura*, which ran articles mocking and belittling the Tutsi, and cartoons strangely reminiscent of Nazi cartoons about the Jews in the 1930s. *Kangura's* anti-Tutsi articles were read aloud at public gatherings to reach the illiterate.

Kangura stopped printing shortly before the genocide. Phase 2 was begun with the 1993 launch of Radio-Television Libre des Mille Collines, or RTLM. Founded by the same extremists within the government and funded by the same businessmen who had funded *Kangura*, RTLM replaced *Kangura* as the primary propaganda platform. It used street language, comedy, pop music and phone-ins to appeal to the youth, particularly aiming for the unemployed, the delinquents, and the illiterate. It quickly became propagandistic, with false news stories, talk shows twisting events, mockery and ridicule of the Tutsis, building to an outright call for extermination of the Tutsis.

RTLM recruited the militia that would do the bidding of the extremist Hutus. It created the Rwandan version of the Nazi brown shirts. Between January 1993 and March 1994, millionaire Félicien Kabuga, one of the funders of both *Kangura* and RTLM, simultaneously imported 500,000 machetes in preparation for what was to come[127].

On April 6, 1994, a plane carrying Rwandan president Juvénal Habyarimana and Burundian president Cyprien Ntaryamira was shot out of the sky with surface-to-air missiles as it prepared to land in the Rwandan capital of

Kigali. They were returning from peace negotiations with the Tutsi. A half hour after the crash, the militia members set up checkpoints in the cities and the killing began.

Once the first blood was spilled, RTLM served as an accelerant, broadcasting license plates and addresses of Tutsi targets and moderate Hutus, urging listeners to "keep killing" as "the graves are not yet full," and even broadcasting "music to kill by." At the checkpoints and on the roads, young men held machetes or assault rifles in one hand and a radio, tuned to RTLM, in another. When it was over, 70% of the Tutsi, and an uncounted number of moderate Hutus, were dead.

It was a diminutive, brilliant historian and senior advisor to Human Rights Watch from Brooklyn, Alison Des Forge, who first brought Mucchielli's *Psychologie de la publicité et de la propagande* to public attention. With a PhD in history from Yale and a MacArthur Genius Award to her credit, Des Forge was widely considered the world's foremost authority on the Rwanda genocide. Her book, *Leave None to Tell the Story: Genocide in Rwanda*, published in 1999, is recognized as the definitive work on the genocide.

In *Leave None to Tell the Story*, Des Forge makes a note of a discovery by her research team:

> In a mimeographed document entitled *Note Relative à la Propagande d'Expansion et de Recrutement*, found in Butare prefecture, one propagandist tells others how to sway the public most effectively. Obviously someone who had studied at university level, the author of the note presents a

detailed analysis of a book called *Psychologie de la publicité et de la propagande* by Roger Mucchielli, published in Paris in 1970.

The author of the note claims to convey lessons learned from the book and drawn from Lenin and Goebbels. He advocates using lies, exaggeration, ridicule, and innuendo to attack the opponent, in both his public and his private life. He suggests that moral considerations are irrelevant, except when they happen to offer another weapon against the other side. He adds that it is important not to underestimate the strength of the adversary nor to overestimate the intelligence of the general public targeted by the campaign. Propagandists must aim both to win over the uncommitted and to cause divisions among supporters of the other point of view. They must persuade the public that the adversary stands for war, death, slavery, repression, injustice, and sadistic cruelty.[128]

Des Forges notes that the propagandists in Rwanda regularly used the techniques described in Mucchielli's book. It was reading her notes that sent me in search of *Psychologie de la publicité et de la propagande*. Without Alison Des Forges, it is very possible we would never have had access to the information Mucchielli was trying to pass on.

MYANMAR

In 2013 Myanmar was a fledgling democracy, having emerged only five years earlier from rule by a brutal military junta. In the transition to democracy, the military, the Tatmadaw, retained power over some areas of the government, and held seats in the new parliament. Now five years in, they weren't happy with the way democracy was working out. The National League for Democracy (NLD), a party they had worked for decades to suppress, was achieving overwhelming popularity. So the old generals came up with a plan.

With the loosening of the reins by the junta in the previous years, European telecom companies had been allowed to compete in the Myanmar market. Sales of smart phones with Internet access were beginning to explode. Between 2013 and 2018, the number of people in Myanmar connected online through their phones would go from 1.2 million to 18 million. 86% of online users were on Facebook. A 2016 report by GSMA, the global body representing mobile operators, found that, in Myanmar, for many people Facebook was the only online entry point for information; many regarded Facebook postings as real news.

Myanmar's Department of Defense hired 700 staff to utilize this new resource, and put them to work in hidden offices around the capital, surreptitiously creating and posting to fake Facebook pages. They started with fan pages for celebrities and military heroes to build the numbers. Then, because every good propaganda campaign needs a scapegoat, they used the pages and other fake accounts to begin spewing hatred toward the Muslim Rohingya, a tiny 4% minority in a country that is 94% Buddhist. The

Rohingya had been in Myanmar for centuries.

The propagandists flooded users' Facebook feeds with doctored and faked photos of supposed atrocities by the Rohingya and calls for violent retribution. One fabricated story said that "mosques in Yangon are stockpiling weapons in an attempt to blow up various Buddhist religious sites, including the 2,500-year-old Shwedagon Pagoda, the most sacred Buddhist pagoda in Myanmar.

A post from 2013 featured a restaurant advertisement featuring Rohingya-style food, with text saying "We must fight them the way Hitler did the Jews, damn kalars!" using a pejorative for the Rohingya. Other examples from among the thousands posted in the course of the campaign: "These non-human kalar dogs, the Bengalis, are killing and destroying our land, our water and our ethnic people. We need to destroy their race," and next to photos of a boatload of Rohingya refugees landing in Indonesia, "Pour fuel and set fire so that they can meet Allah faster."[129]

A baby-faced Buddhist monk, Ashin Wirathu, became the "face" of the military's campaign, building and leading a band of other extremist monks stoking fears of a Muslim takeover of Myanmar. The Muslim "dogs," he said, were "stealing our women, raping them," and had the goal to take over the country and destroy Buddhism, its culture, and its values. The NLD, he said, was secretly supporting a Muslim agenda. In 2013, just about the time I was seeing posts and emails in rural California saying Obama was the leader of the "Muslim takeover of America," Wirathu was telling his followers that President Obama had been "tainted by black Muslim blood." He claimed that the UN had been hijacked by Arabs and that around 90% of Muslims in Myanmar were "radical bad people." Finally, he warned that "taking care of our religion and race is more important than democracy."[130]

The campaign began with a widespread boycott of Muslim businesses and escalated to Buddhist mobs burning Rohingya businesses and villages and killing hundreds of Rohingya. In several instances, monks were seen goading-on frenzied Buddhists. The Tatmadaw began rounding up the Rohingya and confining them to camps where they were not allowed to leave to work or attend to their shops and were denied basic medical needs or education.

In 2017, 150 Rohingya attacked 24 police stations, security outposts, and an army base in the Rakhine region, in what the attackers claimed was a response to the atrocities committed on their communities. They were quickly put down. By the end of the day, 59 insurgents and 12 members of the security forces were killed.

The trigger was pulled. Mobs of Buddhists in the region, now joined and led by military forces, descended on the Rohingya communities in the region in a murderous frenzy. There are multiple eyewitness accounts of Buddhists and members of the security forces hacking Rohingya men, women, and children to death, and raping Rohingya women in front of their families before killing them. According to Doctors Without Borders, at least 6,700 Rohingya were killed between August 25 and September 24 (other sources reported that it was over 24,000). Roughly 600,000 fled the region to Bangladesh, where they remain in squalid refugee camps.

Facebook had received reports and complaints about the misinformation, the incitement to violence, and even pornographic anti-Muslim Facebook posts for more than five years before they shut down the fake accounts in 2018—nearly a year after the worst of the violence and mass murder. It was hard, they said, to find enough translators to monitor posts.

Four years after the murderous ethnic cleansing of the Rohingya communities, Myanmar held a new parliamentary election. Perhaps the generals thought that having saved the nation from the Rohingya "threat" would endear them to the voters. Again, it didn't work out well for them. The election results further advanced the NLD and resulted in a loss of parliamentary seats by the party of the Tatmadaw. The generals had what has now become a familiar response. They declared the election fraudulent and staged a coup.

As though on cue, Wirathu's nationalist Buddhist monks launched Facebook campaigns and staged demonstrations, carrying banners proclaiming that the election had been stolen by the NLD. The Tatmadaw quickly imprisoned the country's democratic leaders and seized control of the country. When the streets filled with protesters, they simply mowed them down with guns. More than 3,000 unarmed civilians, mostly of them young democracy activists, were murdered in the streets by the country's military or taken away to prison where many more perished. As they died, so did Myanmar's democracy.

As mentioned earlier in the text, a note in the *New York Times* on October 15, 2018 noted that the officers involved in the Myanmar operation had studied psychological warfare in Moscow. When they came back, they had delivered lectures to others on what they had learned. Myanmar's military had been sending groups of its officers to Russia for military training since 2000.[131]

ACKNOWLEDGMENTS

People tell stories of meeting someone and thinking, "That's the man (or woman) I'm going to marry." When I met José Ramos-Horta in 2001, I thought, "That's the man I'm going to work with." I have been somewhere in his vicinity since, through the birth his nation, Timor-Leste, as the millennium's newest democracy in 2002, the civil conflict of 2006, his first term as president in 2007, in the safe house with him and his family after he was shot, during his current term as president, and points in between. He has always had faith in me and for that I'm grateful.

Two women, Bonnie Abaunza and Kathy Wattman, each conquer the world on a daily basis in their work; their strength and the generosity of spirit they demonstrate in the lives they touch, including mine, have kept me going forward. This book would not have happened without them.

David Kline, Corinne Simon-Duneau, Tim Rosaire, and Marty Kassowitz believed in this book, and in me, from the beginning, when it counts the most.

I used to have a bookmark with Garfield the Cat on it (and I know this dates me). It said, "I live like I type – fast with a lot of mistakes." So, after the manuscript was proofread, Marty, Corinne and Glenn Ballentine proofread it again. And again. For this you can be grateful.

ENDNOTES

1   Fritz Stern, "German Big Business and the Rise of Hitler." *Foreign Affairs Magazine*, April 19, 2022.

2   Roger Mucchielli, *Psychologie de la Publicité et de la Propagande*, (Paris, Libraries Techniques, Entreprise Moderne D'Edition et Les Editions E.S.F., 1970), 22.

3   William H. Tucker, *The Cattell Controversy : Race, Science, and Ideology*. (Chicago, University of Illinois Press, March 2009).

4   *In Memory of Wilhelm Wundt by His American Students,* (The Psychological Review, Vol 28, No 3, May, 1921) 134.

5   Mucchielli, 22.

6   Mucchielli, 20.

7   Mucchielli, 20.

8   Clyde Miller, *The Process of Persuasion*, (New York, Crown Publishers, 1946).

9   Miller, 21.

10   Gustave Le Bon, *The Crowd: A Study of the Popular Mind*. (Chump Change, 1896) Kindle edition, 43 - 46.

11   Le Bon, 43 - 46.

12   Le Bon, 59.

13   Le Bon, 56.

14   Le Bon, 167.

15   Le Bon, 167

16   Gustave Le Bon, The *Influence of Race in History* (Review Scientifique, April 28, 1888).

17   Ibid.

18   Geoff Eley, *Citizenship and National Identity in Twentieth-Century Germany* (Palo Alto, Stanford University Press, 2007) 284.

19   Gerhard L. Weinberg and Jay Y. Gonen. "The Roots of Nazi Psychology: Hitler's Utopian Barbarism." *German Studies Review* 24, no. 1, February 1, 2001, 210.

20   Le Bon, 37.

21   Edward Bernays, *Propaganda*. (Brooklyn, NY: Ig Publishing, 2004), 47.

22   Stuart Ewen, *PR, A Social History of Spin*, (New York, Basic Books. 1996.

23   Bernays, 10.

24   Bernays, 50.

25   Louis Pizzitola, *Hearst Over Hollywood*.(New York, Columbia University Press, 2002).

26   Marvin Olasky, "Reception of Edward Bernays' Doctrine of 'Manipulating Public Opinion," University of Texas, 1984.https://files.eric.ed.gov/fulltext/ED245231.pdf

27   Scott M. Cutlip, *The Unseen Power: Public Relations: A History.* (Taylor & Francis, 2013).

28   Mucchielli, 3.

29   Mucchielli, 27.

30   Mucchielli, 30.

31   Mucchielli, 77.

32   Mucchielli, 77.

33   Mucchielli, 30.

34   Mucchielli, 79.

35   Mucchielli, 79.

36   Mucchielli, 78.

37   Mucchielli, 80.

38   Mucchielli, 80.

39   US Flag Code, Military.com, August 30, 2021, https://www.military.com/flag-day/us-flag-code.html.

40   Le Bon, 60.

41   Mucchielli, 80.

42   Mucchielli, 21.

43   Le Bon, 94.

44   Mucchielli, 80-81.

45   Mucchielli, 80-81.

46   Mucchielli, 80-81.

47   René Girard, *The Scapegoat* (Baltimore, The Johns Hopkins University Press, 1989).

48   Paul Fauconnet, "La responsabilité" (French Edition, January 1, 1920).

49   Mucchielli, 90.

50   "Prisoners of the Camps," *United States Holocaust Memorial Museum*, n.d., https://encyclopedia.ushmm.org/content/en/article/prisoners-of-the-camps

51   Mucchielli, 66.

52   Mucchielli, 91.

53   Mucchielli, 78,

54   Mucchielli, 89,

55   Mucchielli, 90,

56   Alexandra Hutzler, "Read Donald Trump's Statement After Liz Cheney Ousted From GOP Leadership," *Newsweek*, May 12, 2021.

57   Robert Citino, PhD, "Meet the Freikorps: Vanguard of Terror 1918-1923," *Military History Magazine*, November, 2012, cited by the National WW II Museum.

58   Citino, "Meet the Freikorps: Vanguard of Terror *1918-1923*".

59   Nigel Jones, *A Brief History of the Birth of the Nazis* (London: Robinson, 2004) 151.

60   André François-Poncet, *The Fateful Years: Memoirs of a French Ambassador in Berlin, 1931–1938*, trans. Jacques LeClercq (New York: Harcourt Brace, 1949), 48.

61   Melita Maschmann, *Account Rendered: A Dossier on My Former Self*, trans. Geoffrey Strachan (London: Abelard-Schuman, 1965), 9.

62   "The SA," *United States Holocaust Memorial Museum*, n.d., https://encyclopedia.ushmm.org/content/en/article/the-sa

63   Richard Evans, *The Coming of the Third Reich* (New York, Penguin Group, 2004) Kindle edition) 454.

64   "Former Nazi Torture and Detention Sites Uncovered in Germany." *The World*, August 15, 2013, https://theworld.org/stories/2013-05-06/former-nazi-torture-and-detention-sites-uncovered-germany

65   "Kemna, Das bergische Konzentrationslager 1933-1934," *Kemna-Erinnern*, n.d., https://en.kemna-erinnern.de/informations.html

66   Evans, 454

67   Richard Evans, "The Conspiracists," *London Review of Books,* May 8, 2014.

68   Joachim C. Fest, *Hitler*, (New York, Harcourt Brace Jovanovich, 1974), p 397

69   Ibid

70   "Reichstag Fire Decree," *United States Holocaust Memorial Museum*, n.d, https://encyclopedia.ushmm.org/content/en/timeline-event/holocaust/1933-1938/reichstag-fire-decree

71   Joseph Goebbels: Two Speeches on the Tasks of the Reich Ministry for Popular Enlightenment and Propaganda, (March 15 / March 25, 1933), *German History in Documents and Images.*, n.d., https://germanhistorydocs.org/en/nazi-germany-1933-1945/joseph-goebbels-two-speeches-on-the-tasks-of-the-reich-ministry-for-popular-enlightenment-and-propaganda-march-15-march-25-1933

72   Ralf Georg Reuth, *Goebbels,* (Boston, Mariner Books, 1994), cited in Evans, Richard, The Coming of the

Third Reich, 396

73   Evans, 396

74   Ibid

75   "Deluig Tonwoche," cited by *United States Holocaust Memorial Museum*, n.d. https://encyclopedia.ushmm.org/content/en/film/reichstag-fire-trial

76   Evans, 426

77   Ibid

78   Mucchielli, 88

79   Mucchielli, 88

80   Mucchielli, 88

81   Mucchielli, 92

82   "Statement from the University of Cambridge about Dr. Aleksandr Kogan," *University of Cambridge*, October 12, 2023, https://www.cam.ac.uk/notices/news/statement-from-the-university-of-cambridge-about-dr-aleksandr-kogan

83   Julia Carrie and Paul Lewis, "Facebook gave data about 57bn friendships to academic," *The Guardian*, March 22, 2018.

84   Irani, Delshad, "Why is ex-adman Nigel Oakes being hailed as the '007' of big data?," *The Economic Times,* March 29, 2017.

85   Irani, Delshad, "Why is ex-adman Nigel Oakes being

hailed as the '007' of big data?

86   Jamie Doward and Alice Gibbs, "Did Cambridge Analytica influence the Brexit vote and the US election?," *The Guardian,* March 4, 2017.

87   Jeremy Dyck, "The Man Behind Cambridge Analytica," *BC Digest*, October 5, 2019, Republished on *Medium.*

88   Bob Dreyfuss, "Cambridge Analytica's PsyOps Warriors," *Rolling Stone*, March 21, 2018.

89   Peter Grant, "Strategic Communication Laboratories and the Mysterious Origins of Cambridge Analytica," *Medium*, September 23, 2023.

90   Jamie Doward and Alice Gibbs, "Did Cambridge Analytica influence the Brexit vote and the US election?,"

91   Sharon Weinberger, "You Can't Handle the Truth, Psy-Ops Propaganda Goes Mainstream," *Slate.com*, Sept 19, 2005.

92   Ellen Barry, "Long Before Cambridge Analytica, a Belief in the 'Power of the Subliminal,'" *New York Times,* April 20, 2018.

93   "SCL influence in foreign elections, Disinformation and 'fake news,' Final Report," UK Parliament., https://publications.parliament.uk/pa/cm201719/cmselect/cmcumeds/1791/179110.htm

94   David Brown, "Nigel Oakes, the low-profile link to Cambridge Analytica, copied Aristotle and Hitler," *The Economic Times,* March 21, 2018.

95   Briant, Emma L., "Three Explanatory Essays Giving Context and Analysis to Submitted Evidence." Published by UK Parliament, Mar 18, 2018.

96   Ibid.

97   Ibid.

98   Ibid.

99   Ibid.

100   "United States of America before the Federal Trade Commission, in the Matter of Cambridge Analytica," Docket Number 9383, FTC.gov, July 24, 2019, https://www.parliament.uk/globalassets/documents/commons-committees/culture-media-and-sport/Dr-Emma-Briant-Explanatory-Essays.pdf

101   Vincent Bielski, "Renaissance Partner Airs Battle With Mercer Over Trump", *Forbes*, February 23, 2017.

102   Carole Cadwalladr, "I made Steve Bannon's psychological warfare tool': meet the data war whistleblower," *The Guardian,* March 18, 2018.

103   Andy Kroll, Cloak and Data: The Real Story Behind Cambridge Analytica's Rise and Fall" Mother Jones Magazine, May/June 2018

104   Tom Cheshire, "Behind the scenes at Donald Trump's UK digital war room," *Sky News*, 27 November 2018.

105   Wylie, Christopher, "Written Statement to the United States Senate Committee on the Judiciary, In the Matter of

Cambridge Analytica and Other Related Issues," United States Senate Committee on the Judiciary, May 16, 2018, https://www.judiciary.senate.gov/imo/media/doc/05-16-18%20Wylie%20Testimony.pdf

106   Ibid.

107   Ibid.

108   Sam Schechner, Jenny Gross, Rebecca Balhaus, "Cambridge Analytica CEO Promised More Than He Delivered, Clients Say," *Wall Street Journal,* March 28, 2018.

109   Kroll, Andy, "Cloak and Data: The Real Story Behind Cambridge Analytica's Rise and Fall"

110   Carole Cadwalladr and Lee Glendinning, "Exposing Cambridge Analytica: 'It's been exhausting, exhilarating, and slightly terrifying,'" *The Guardian,* September 29, 2018.

111   Alex Isenstadt, "Trump campaign hires alum of controversial data company," *Politico,* February 19, 2020.

112   "Investigation into the use of data analytics in political campaigns, a report to Parliament, Information Commissioner's Office, November 6, 2018, https://ico.org.uk/media/action-weve-taken/2260271/investigation-into-the-use-of-data-analytics-in-political-campaigns-final-20181105.pdf

113   "The Great Hack's David Carrol finally sees his Cambridge Analytica data," Channel 4 News, September 29, 2020.

114   Stephanie Kirchgaessner, Manisha Ganguly, David Pegg, Carole Cadwalladr, and Jason Burke, "Revealed: the

hacking and disinformation team meddling in elections," *The Guardian*, February 14, 2023.

115   Samantha Bradshaw, Hannah Bailey, and Phillip N Howard, "Industrialized Disinformation 2020 Global Inventory of Organized Social Media Manipulation," Computational Propaganda Research Project, *Oxford Internet Institute and University of Oxford*, n.d., https://demtech.oii.ox.ac.uk/wp-content/uploads/sites/12/2021/01/CyberTroop-Report-2020-v.2.pdf

116   Jason Daley, "Popular social media mobile apps extract data from photos on your phone...", College of Engineering, University of Wisconsin-Madison, Apil 2, 2024, https://engineering.wisc.edu/news/popular-social-media-mobile-apps-extract-data-from-photos-on-your-phone-introducing-both-bias-and-errors/

117   Vonnegut, Kurt, letter to Xavier High School and Ms. Lockwood, November 5, 2006, cited by Cynthia Haven, The Book Haven, Stanford University, https://bookhaven.stanford.edu/2022/05/kurt-vonneguts-advice-to-students-dance-home-after-school-make-a-face-in-your-mashed-potatoes-pretend-youre-count-dracula/

118   Gibson, James L., "Mass Opposition to the Soviet Putsch of August 1991: Collective Action, Rational Choice, and Democratic Values in the Former Soviet Union," September 1997, The American Political Review

119   Dobbs, Michael, "Protesters Confront Tanks in Moscow," *The Washington Post,* August 20, 1991.

120   Taomo Zhou, "Ambivalent Alliance: Chinese Policy towards Indonesia, 1960–1965," *Cambridge Core, Cambridge University Press*, February 11, 2015

121   Paul Lashmar, James Oliver, "*Britain's Secret Propaganda War: Foreign Office and the Cold War, 1948–77,*" . Stroud, Gloucestershire, Sutton Pub, Ltd., 1999.

122   Paul Lashmar, Nicholas Gilby and James Oliver, "UK's propaganda leaflets inspired 1960s massacre of Indonesian communists," *The Guardian*, January 23, 2022

123   Bradley Simpson, "The United States and the 1965–1966 Mass Murders in Indonesia," *Monthly Review*, December 1, 2015

124   Vincent Bevins, "What the United States Did in Indonesia," *The Atlantic*, October 20, 2017

125   Telegram 868 from Jakarta to State, October 5, 1965; and Telegram 851 from Jakarta to State, October 5, 1965, both in RG 59, Central Files, 1964–1966, POL 23-9, Indonesia, NA; Ralph McGehee, "The CIA and the White Paper on El Salvador," *Nation*, April 11, 1981.

126   Vincent Bevins, "What the United States Did in Indonesia."

127   Amy Goodman, "Human Rights Investigator and Rwandan Expert Alison Des Forges Dies in New York Plane Crash." *Democracy Now*. February 16, 2009.

128   Martin Meredith, *The State of Africa*, (London, Simon and Schuster UK, 2006)

129   Alison Liebhafsky Des Forge, *Leave None to Tell the Story: Genocide in Rwanda* (New York, Human Rights Watch, 1999)

130   Steve Stecklow, "Why Facebook is losing the war on hate speech in Myanmar," Reuters, August 15, 2018.

131   Paul Mozur, A Genocide Incited on Facebook, With Posts From Myanmar's Military, *New York Times*, October 15, 2018.

Photo by Ray Kachatorian

Since 2001 **Mary Wald** has been writing and editing articles and speeches, and producing media, for Nobel Peace Prize laureates, including Archbishop Desmond Tutu, former Presidents Mikhail Gorbachev and Jimmy Carter, and His Holiness the Dalai Lama. She has initiated and authored joint actions by the laureates on critical social issues including the use of torture by the US, the execution of dissidents by Saudi Arabia, the persecution of journalists in the Philippines, and more. Twenty-seven Nobel laureates have taken part in her initiatives, which have been covered by the Associated Press, the *New York Times, Washington Post, Chicago Tribune, Los Angeles Times, Wall Street Journal*, and more.

She is the international media representative for José Ramos-Horta, winner of the 1996 Nobel Peace Prize and current President of Timor-Leste, and has been a contributor to the online news publications *Huffington Post* and *The Hill*.

www.ingramcontent.com/pod-product-compliance
Lightning Source LLC
Chambersburg PA
CBHW020538030426
42337CB00013B/898